To EH

in Memory of 'Poppy'
Peter A Bond Nov 8, 1934
            to Sept 22, 2012

This is one of Poppy's
'Fishing and Wild Life books

Enjoy   **The Master Angler**
        Love
        Grammy Marcia
                Oct, 2012

The Master Angler

using color technology to catch more fish

Phil Rabideau

hancock

house

ISBN 0-88839-561-2
Copyright © 2004 Phillip A. Rabideau

Cataloging in Publication Data
Rabideau, Phil, 1928-
    The master angler : using color technology to catch more
fish / Phil Rabideau.

ISBN 0-88839-561-2

1. Fishing lures. 2. Lure fishing. I. Title.

SH449.R32 2004   799.12   C2004-902224-5

All rights reserved. No part of this publication may be reproduced, stored
in a retrieval system or transmitted, in any form or by any means,
electronic, mechanical, photocopying, recording, or otherwise, without the
prior written permission of Hancock House Publishers.

Printed in China - JADE

Cover Design: Rick Groenheyde
Production & Book Design: Theodora Kobald & Rick Groenheyde
Editor: Yvonne Lund
Photo Credits: All fishermen photographs courtesy of Mepps.

Published simultaneously in Canada and the United States by

HANCOCK HOUSE PUBLISHERS LTD.
19313 Zero Avenue, Surrey, B.C. V3S 9R9
(604) 538-1114 Fax (604) 538-2262

HANCOCK HOUSE PUBLISHERS
1431 Harrison Avenue, Blaine, WA 98230-5005
(604) 538-1114 Fax (604) 538-2262
Web Site: www.hancockhouse.com *email:* sales@hancockhouse.com

Contents

This book is dedicated to my family

To my wife Bonnie, who has indulged my fishing habit for over 50 years.

To my son Mike, who has been my fishing buddy for almost 50 years.

And to daughter Sandy, who has made me a very proud father.

It is dedicated too, to the Sheldons, the late Todd Sheldon who brought Mepps to

North America, and to Mike Sheldon, the present owner of Mepps Sheldons' Inc.

They have made my retirement years better than I ever thought they could be.

To Dr. Judith Stowe, who tutored me in the foundations of

behavioral psychology and animal behavior.

To Colin Kageyama, O.D., who pioneered the application of color technology

to fishing lures and co designed the See Best™ line of spinners.

And to all the great Mepps Sheldons' employees with whom

I have worked for the last fifteen years.

Finally, to "Rab," my dad, and the Boy Scouts for giving me my

moral compass, and to my high school math and science teacher,

Esther Rice, who started me on the path to learning.

Foreword

Mark Plath.
Walleye.

A Fishing Odyssey

Fishing—to me—is a labor of love. The purpose of this book is to teach a person how to become a Master Angler, and enjoy this wonderful sport even more. I hope to offer you a sensible, more productive and enjoyable way to approach fishing. There is so much commercialism, less-than-honest claims and self interest in fishing today. Plus, the majority of fishing advice cannot withstand the scrutiny of disciplined investigation. Finding something straightforward, based on research, and proven by experience may be refreshing for a change. This book has a scientific underpinning, but what has been set forth has been verified by anecdotal situations in which the author personally took part, over many years. By adopting our prescribed approach, your catch rate will improve markedly.

Humble beginnings

My first recollection of fishing was on Oswego Lake, then on the outskirts of Portland, Oregon, circa 1930. I was two then. It was the start of the Great Depression and work was really scarce. So one day, Dad took brother Jim, Jerry (our bull dog) and me fishing. It is amazing, some seventy years later, what you recall when it comes to fishing. I remember the wooden row boat—don't think outboards were even around then, but who could have afforded them anyway? We had cane poles, a red and green cork bobber, braided silk line, hook and sinker and the universal lure of the time, a can of angle worms. Would you believe I still have that red and green bobber? It sits in front of me while I write this book as a reminder of what fishing is all about. Being with your dad, family dog and a pal, out of doors on a lake with just you and gifts of Mother Nature is as good as it gets. We had the time of our lives with our cane pole rigs and a can of worms. Once we had a stringer of perch, we headed home, hand in hand, proud as peacocks.

We moved to Bonneville Dam in 1936, on the Columbia River, where my electrician dad helped construct the dam. Talk about going to heaven at an early age, talk about a chance to be a Huckleberry Finn. The summers were enchanting, except my mother made brother and I bucksaw and split wood each day, for heating and cooking, before we could head for the river. Once that was done, we grabbed our poles and our .22 rifle and headed out to our Columbia, a short walk down the road.

Except for the salmon runs, we fished a half dozen creeks that tumble down the sides of the famous Columbia River Gorge. To get where we were going, we walked the Union Pacific railroad tracks. Our fishing tackle was hollow steel, telescoping rods and casting reels. The reels were not level wind, and the handles spun around when we cast. We learned fast about "bird nests." Our bait was a flat, pocket-sized Prince Albert tobacco can full of freshly-dug angle worms. And, if we could find enough pop bottles by the side of the roads, we could turn them in for a jar of salmon eggs. Those were golden days, in the heart of the Depression to which we were oblivious. I only knew later that there was a Depression, because when I looked at my fifth grade picture, all the boys had knee patches on their overalls.

From Bonneville, we moved in 1939 to Grand Coulee Dam where dad worked for years on the dam. These were war years, and even if you had money, there was nothing to buy. Plus, money was to be saved and not spent—the reverse of today's generation.

I remember my second fishing rod to this day. After mowing lawns for a summer, I hid away enough money to buy a fly rod. This was well before spinning tackle, even monofilament lines. Anyway, the local hardware store had a Shakespeare rod, line and reel set. Well, I had my eye on it for weeks; a three-piece, nine-foot bamboo rod and matching Medalist reel...wow! The set cost eleven dollars. I could wait no longer as the summer was almost over. When I got it home, my dear mother, Edna, asked the sixty-four- dollar question: "What did you pay for it?" With head down, I said, "Eleven dollars, Mother." We did not have rockets in those days, but she got into orbit very quickly. I can still hear dear little mother shouting "ELEVEN DOLLARS!" Next was "CLARENCE!" (When there was trouble astir, dad was Clarence, but most of the time he was Rab.) Rab was the greatest dad a kid ever had. He helped me through many of these ordeals, as mother thought fishing tackle was a luxury we could not afford.

We always had our rods with us while we were backpacking on the weekends, and fishing was reliably good on the nearby Nez Pierce Indian reservation. In those days, there were even largemouth bass in Steamboat Rock Lake (now flooded and Banks Lake) near Grand Coulee Dam. We could not afford hip boots—and waders, we never heard of such things. So, we bass fished with cutoffs and tennis shoes along the cat tails. By this time we had broken our trusty old telescoping rods and moved on to steel casting rods (but with the same old casting reels). My buddy Mike Mays and I fished with his dad Slim, from Oklahoma, who knew all the good stuff about bass fishing. Only three of us could go, because we only had three wooden bass lures—a Pike Minnow, a Heddon Mouse and a Heddon Crazy Crawler. We would take turns using a given lure. In the Northwest, bass were considered trash fish by fishermen, in those days. But war-time meat rationing was on. I remember one day we caught a gunny sack full of bass. Catch and release was from a practical standpoint fifty years off, so the neighborhood had fresh fish for dinner. Most of them had never tasted bass, nor heard of them.

There were no smallmouth bass in those days, as they were introduced by bringing them to the Columbia from the East by rail in the late 1800s and planted down where the Snake River joins the Columbia. Now largemouth and smallmouth bass are major fisheries in the Northwest, due to the decline in the salmon fisheries. Bass clubs and tournaments abound.

Walleye were introduced in the 70s behind the many dams built on the Columbia, and they have migrated all the way down to tidewater. The Columbia is now one of the major walleye fisheries in the country. Walleye clubs and tournaments are also plentiful. Unfortunately, the salmon lobbies have convinced the Game departments that walleye eat major amounts of salmon smolt (which is not true). The walleye fishery is now hurting because of politics—not to mention the Native Americans being able to catch them "accidentally" in their salmon gillnets and set lines...but I digress.

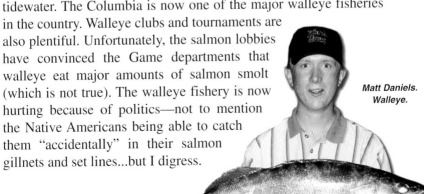

Matt Daniels.
Walleye.

On hold

After a brief stint in the Navy (WWII was over), I earned my electrical engineering degree from the University of Washington in Seattle. I mention this, because to be a competent engineer, you must be analytical, and stick to fundamentals and the laws of physics. The same is true with being a good fisherman. Most fishermen learn fishing by "trial and error"—mostly "error." Fishermen can get away with that approach, but engineers can't. Not only does it end your engineering career, but in the meantime, you can kill people. You will find a lot of "engineering" in this book.

In my senior year in engineering school, I met Bonnie, now my wife of 50 plus years. She was a graduate home economist from Iowa State and a stewardess for Northwest Airlines—a great combination—who has been a wonderful wife, companion and home manager. She has always let me do my "fishing" thing, but has never understood why guys need so much fishing gear. I always said "When I have as much tackle as you have shoes, perfume and purses, I will stop accumulating fishing gear."...It's a guy and girl thing.

After my graduation in 1951 we headed east with a major electrical company, for whom I worked thirty-five years. We pledged that we would get back to the Northwest in five years, but it took forty-five years to get home. But I do not regret one bit my time in the East. I had assignments in Cincinnati, Detroit, Pittsburgh and Austin (Texas). And you know, there is good fishing all over the country. My fishing was on hold until we got to Michigan in 1955. Michigan is the place to be, if you are a fisherman, and Canada is close by.

Back at it

When we got to Michigan, the first thing I did was to have dad send me my old trusty bamboo fly rod. My engineering manager in Detroit was Frank Fennell, who has turned out to be a cherished friend and a Michigan and Canada fishing buddy. Frank was from Pennsylvania, and an ardent trout fisherman. Frank lives in Edina, Minnesota now, and still fly-fishes on the west side of Wisconsin.

Jack Bishop. Striper.

Michigan is surrounded by the Great Lakes and has literally thousands of lakes and famous trout streams, like the Au Sable and the Betsy. Great camping and canoeing country too. And with the salmon and steelhead introduced in the Great Lakes in the mid-sixties, Michigan went from great to outstanding from a fisherman's standpoint. The stream fishing is altogether different in Michigan than the West, as the streams are slower and travel through sandy geology on the way to the Great Lakes. Son Mike was born in Cincinnati and Sandy arrived soon after we moved to Michigan. We had a tent camper trailer and a Brittany spaniel, Tillie. We saved up our money and bought a twelve-foot Alumacraft car top boat and a six hp Mercury outboard. We camped every summer , at a wonderful State Park, always on a lake, of course. Mike, Sandy, Tillie and I spent joyous days in our little boat while Bonnie read and enjoyed the beaches. I have a feeling that a family that camps and fishes together, stays together.

On to Pennsylvania

While in the Detroit area, I earned my MBA and was transferred to corporate headquarters in Pittsburgh. And, would you know it, Pennsylvania has some fine fishing too. The Allegheny River and Susquehanna River basins are great Pennsylvania fisheries where smallmouth and trout are king. We still had the tent camper trailer, and enjoyed our state park camping routine in Pennsylvania and New York . The premier of all family camping spots is Lake George State Park in upper NY state, where you camp on islands, and have your own dock, tent platform and outdoor john. The water is so pure, you could drink it right out of the lake. There, I caught my first smallmouth, which was over five pounds.

eve Crowley. Steelhead.

11

Randy Polisky. Largemouth bass.

When in Pittsburgh, our son Mike went to the Naval Academy to start his Navy career as a carrier pilot. Every chance we had, we would get together for a fishing expedition.

On to Texas

Now if you haven't done the largemouth bass gig in Texas, you have really missed something—Lakes Sam Rayburn, Toledo Bend, and Lake Fork for starters. In Texas, only one of the lakes is natural, Caddo Lake, and if you wish to fish amongst the cypress, this is it. All the rivers in Texas run generally from the NW to SE, and have at least one dam on them. They all end up in the Gulf of Mexico where fishing for "reds" (red drum) and sea trout (weakfish) abound. You learn quickly how to fish reservoirs, with lots of submerged live oak trees.

We moved to Austin, with its State Capitol and the University of Texas (Hook 'em Horns!), where pickup trucks far outnumber everything else. Texas is the home of barbecue, TexMex food, Willie Nelson and the Texas two-step. And, in the 70s they could spot a "Yankee" a mile off. At the plant picnic, the highlights were the cow-pie and beer (Lone Star) can tossing contests. In the pasture in front of the plant we had two longhorn steers.

The Lower Colorado River runs right through town. Town Lake is the first lake, then Lake Austin (on which I lived within the city limits), Travis, Marble Falls, LBJ and Buchanan all in a row. Besides largemouth, there were stripers, sand bass, swipers (a cross between the two), Guadeloupe bass, small mouth and crappie. I was back to fishing heaven. But bass fishing was kind of a cultural shock, and it took awhile to get the hang of it.

Along with pickup trucks, bass boats are a Texas cultural icon. Even then, they had seventy-five hp motors and seventeen-foot rigs (I hung on for dear life)—a far cry from our six hp, twelve-footer.

All that greeted me when I got to Austin. I had just checked into my office in the plant my first day, when Kenney, the president of the plant bass club came to introduce himself, and invite

Derek Plath. Crappies.

me to be his partner in the monthly tournament on Saturday. The word had gotten out that a new Yankee had come to town, liked to fish and was ready for plucking. I had not seen a largemouth bass in thirty-plus years. Well, I showed up with my single, wimpy, fiberglass, Yankee casting rod with twelve-pound test line and all my new fishing buddies chortled "What is that?!" in chorus. I looked in their boats, and they each had several "pool cue" rods of various lengths and actions, one for worming, flipping or pitching, spinner baits, and crankbaits, with lines that were fifteen to twenty-five pounds. Heck, I did not even understand the bass language— what was I doing there?

Kenney sheepishly showed up, and my bass learning began. I asked what kind of baits we were going to use (they do not say lures in Texas, and plugs are called crank baits), and he said "Spinner Baits or Texas Rigs." I did not know what in the world he was talking about. I found out there were Texas Rigs and Carolina Rigs; but pickup trucks and bass boats were also "rigs", and drilling platforms were called "rigs" as well. Kenney hardly spoke to me all day—this was serious stuff, and he was culling fish in no time. He had pre-fished the lake several days before. I luckily had a similar spinner bait and got plenty of strikes, but only boated one fish late in the day. When I finally had a fish on, and was "playing it out," he said, "If you want to play with the fish, play with it in the boat." After we were back at the launch, I asked Kenney why he caught fish and I had not. He grinned, lifted the skirt of the bait, and there hiding was a "stinger hook." I never had heard of them either. The plucking had started.

Nick Radke.
Largemouth bass.

I fished with the guys in the plant for ten years until I retired. In my second year, I finally won a tournament and became one of the boys.

We lived in Austin for twenty wonderful years—ten working, ten retired. It was in Austin that I began seriously designing fishing lures. When I retired, I became a consultant and lure designer for Mike Sheldon, President of Sheldon's Inc., which owns Mepps USA, Mepps France and Mister Twister. Mike's dad Todd brought the famous French spinner to the United States when he owned a sporting goods store in Antigo, Wisconsin in the late fifties. The Mepps spinner was so successful in the US that Todd eventually purchased Mepps in France and began manufacturing too in Wisconsin. For three generations Mepps has been the "World's Number One Lure."

Back to the Beginning

It took us forty-five years to get back to our roots in the Northwest. In 1996 we moved to Vancouver, Washington, again on the banks of the Columbia. Son Mike now is a Captain for Fed Ex and flies MD11s out of Anchorage. He has a float plane, so guess where I spend a lot of the summer. We have been fishing together now for over forty years. Daughter Sandy still lives in Grand Rapids, Michigan.

Fishing in the Northwest is far different than it was when I left. Fishing in Alaska is not a "gut shot" as you might imagine. A new fishery is always a learning experience. However, by utilizing the principles in this book, you can get up the learning curve fast.

There is no need anymore to ask "What did you catch them on?" or go the "trial and error" route. You probably have seen the T-shirts, "The fisherman with the most lures wins" or " The guy with the biggest bass boat wins." And, would you believe, they are now having bass boat races after tournaments! Time to put things in perspective...hope this book will help. I pledge that following the principles set forth in these pages will allow you to be a better fisherman than you ever thought you could be.

Todd Plath. Walleye.

Introduction

People derive pleasure from fishing for many reasons. But I have yet to meet a fisherman who was not

William Augenti. Atlantic Salmon.

interested in improving his abilities to catch fish. So, for the purposes of this book, fishing is the process of maximizing the probability of catching a targeted fish, under varied conditions. Sounds simple enough, but you need a basic understanding of fish behavior, fish ecology and color technology to become a better than average fisherman. Do not sweat this—we will distill the reams of fish research and fishing information into a usable paradigm, and confirm our approach with various anecdotes. The "experience" factor and "time on the water" are highly overrated. As my colleague Colin Kageyama says, "It is not practice that makes perfect, it is perfect practice that makes perfect." It is like golf. You can spend a lot of time on the practice tee hitting balls, but if you do not know the basics of a good golf swing and the drills to achieve it, you build in a lot of bad habits and never improve. So, too, it is with fishing.

Fish behavior has been studied for well over a hundred years, but the studies are scientific in nature and not accessible in a form that can be readily applied to fishing techniques. The main reason becoming a good fisherman is such a challenge is that the fishermen are deluged with so much unfounded information as well as marketing nonsense. Most manufacturers that make and sell fishing lures know little about the topics of fish behavior, ecology, and color technology. So how can they design an effective lure? They are designing lures for fishermen—not the fish. We must learn those topics ourselves, or continue to fill up our tackle boxes with nonproductive lures.

Most fishermen approach fishing backwards. They start the process by focusing first on the lure—always looking for that "hot" or "fishy" looking lure that is sure to catch fish. Sorry, but there is no such thing as a "magic lure." It may look "fishy" to us, but how does it look to the fish underwater, and how will they react to it? We are enamored with lures that are life-like, even to the extent that they are painted in natural camouflage. Now, does it make sense to buy camouflaged lures so the fish cannot see them? They generally are pricey and tackle boxes are full of them. Again, the manufacturers are focusing on the fisherman and not the fish. Some of the best lures look nothing like natural prey. There are however, a few times when you have to "match the hatch," but that is restricted to specific conditions, which we will cover.

We will reverse the usual lure selection process, and not choose the details of our lure until we arrive at the water. Sometimes the conditions change during the day and we must change lures to suit the changing conditions. If you randomly select a lure from your tackle box, I calculate that you have about a 3% chance of choosing the right one for the conditions—not good odds.

Becoming a good fisherman is like building a brick wall. You have to build it on a solid foundation with one brick at a time. And so it is with fishing. So before we begin thinking about lures, we will learn the physiology of fish, and why they behave the way they do.

Our first chapter is entitled "Your Basic Fish." We will review the sensory abilities of fish: olfactory (smelling), tasting, hearing and seeing. Knowing the physiology of a fish is essential to many things in fishing. Whether you are designing lures, want to cut through the marketplace hype or just become a good fisherman, learning the truth about a fish's sensory makeup is critical.

After we understand the physiology of game fish, we will study why fish behave the way they do in Chapter Two, "Fish Behavior." And, we will learn what makes them bite or strike a lure or bait. It is important to know a fish's eating behavior when selecting a lure. For example, a largemouth bass "slurps" their prey by flaring its gills, passing water through its gill plates and sucking in its prey. More about biting and other related behaviors later.

We then will examine that attributes of fishing lures in Chapter Three, "Lure Attributes" and see how they match-up with the physiology and behavior of our targeted fish. Only then can we be able to select the most effective lure. An effective, "high odds" lure is one that maximizes our chance of catching fish under specified conditions. And, just as important, it will allow us to cull or not buy those "low odds" lures. It will also allow you to disregard the hype of the marketplace.

I imagine by now you are sensing the direction we are heading in this odyssey of learning to be a better fisherman. Selecting lures without first matching them up with the water and sky conditions to be encountered is pure folly.

We have mentioned fish physiology, fish behavior, lure attributes and fishing conditions. Now, we need to combine all these factors, and develop a systematic way of selecting a "high odds" lure. No more "trial and error." On the first cast, we want to have the "high odds" lure on our line.

Chapters Four, Five and Six are devoted to learning about color technology, and how it has a major impact on lure design and selection. Once you have designed a lure to satisfy other attributes, the last thing we do is color and decorate it. But, lure colors seen in the air by the fisherman are not the colors seen by the fish! We will sort that all out for you in Chapter Four. Not only are we to be concerned with the lure's color, but the color of the background upon which the lure is viewed by the fish. And as important, the color of the water. Understanding and applying color technology will by itself make you a far better fisherman.

Chapter Seven is devoted to structure and learning how fish tell time and navigate. Most experienced bass and walleye fishermen already know a lot about structure fishing, which was pioneered in the 60s by the famous Buck Perry. It is helpful to know that fish can tell time and are good navigators.

Chapter Eight was conceived to demystify the "old fishermen's tales" associated with barometers, "dog days", cold fronts, moon tables and tides.

Chapter Nine covers the unique circumstances associated with ponds, lakes, oceans and streams and appropriate techniques for those waters.

This book is primarily about lures, and their selection, but each body of water has its own particular ecological system. We will see in Chapter Ten that lures are designed for particular applications, and there are certain lures that best fit those circumstances.

And finally the last chapter, Chapter Eleven, gets to the bottom line of this book—how to catch more fish by selecting the right lure.

Roger Zeihen. Chinook.

Thomas Wascher. Peacock bass.

Chris Campanelli. Pickerel.

Fishlike vertebrates made their first appearance in the fossil records some 500 to 440 million years ago in the Ordovician period. Fish fossils became very plentiful during the Devonian (the age of fishes) and Carboniferous periods, 395 to 280 million years ago. Dinosaurs did not appear until the Jurassic period, 140 million years ago. To put things in perspective, the first remnants of man are less than two million years old. Some of the ancient fishes we still have around today are sharks, rays, spoonbills, sturgeons and gars. Boney fishes, Teleost, of which we are most interested, became abundant in the Mid Devonian period. Most of our present day game fish appeared in the Cenozoic around 60 million years ago. See Plate 1, a fossil boney fish from Eocene Green River formation, Wyoming some 50 million years old—look familiar?

So why have we reviewed the ancient history of fishes? Because we will find that fish have survived over all these millions of years because of one major factor, their exquisite sensory abilities—far superior to man's. The size of a fish's brain is extraordinarily small, but with their fine sensory abilities, they have changed their behaviors, adapted to the changing world and survived many millions of years. The only real threat to fishes' survival is man!

On to examining the physiology of fishes. Why do we need to know the anatomy of a fish to become a good fisherman? Well, because it will tell you a lot about why fish behave the way they do. And that is a great help in selecting and designing lures.

A major impediment to understanding why fish behave the way

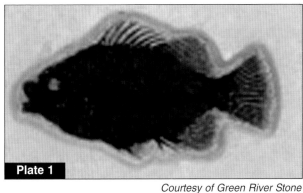

Plate 1

Courtesy of Green River Stone

they do is to describe their actions in human terms. Fish have very small brains. For example, a large northern pike's brain would weigh a fraction of an ounce. Salmon have a brain the size of a pea. "Starting with fishes, and passing upwards through the amphibians and reptiles to the birds and mammals, the region of the brain becomes progressively larger, until in man it forms a very large and important part and its microscopic structure and organization become increasingly complicated."[1] This does not mean that fish do not behave in extraordinary ways. For example, a salmon leaves its birthplace after a year as a smolt, then after three to four years of living in the ocean as a "feeder," returns to its home stream of birth to spawn and die. In human terms, they are not intelligent. But what fish lack in brain capacity, they make up with their extraordinary nervous system, sense organs and senses. That is why they have been around for many millions of years.

Form and fins

There are about 30,0000 species of boney fish in the world, all with different adaptations to their ecology. For the purposes of this book,

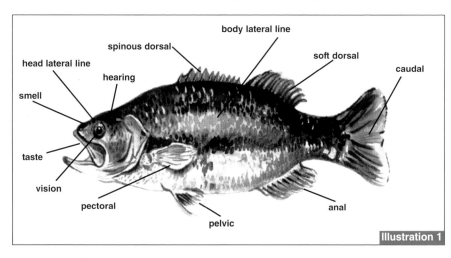

Illustration 1

we will consider typical species that reflect the North American fisheries and the most popular sport fishing families.

Illustration 1 depicts the general form and fin topography of our basic fish. This fish would have average swim speed and be quite maneuverable. The caudal fin (tail), provides the majority of the propulsion power. The spinous dorsal fin is for stability. The pelvic fins are for stability too and counter the buoyancy of the bladder. Some fishes, like the sunfish, use their fins for some propulsion and to swim backwards.

A professional industrial designer has an ingrained rule to obey: "form follows function." And so it is with Mother Nature. The shape of a fish's body is not an arbitrary one, but conforms to hydraulic principles. The hulls of the fast British galleys were patterned after the shape of a mackerel. Submarine hulls, too, conform to fish-like characteristics.

The body of a fish must be unencumbered, and when fish swims fast, their radial fins retract. For speed, a forked tail is more efficient than a truncated or rounded one. The fastest fishes are shaped like skipjack tuna, mackerel and wahoo. A salmon must be very powerful and swim fast under water to be able to exit the water and leap waterfalls to go upstream to spawn. (*Salmo* in Latin means to leap.)

Northern pike and muskellunge are the "clipper ships" of the sports fish, with their elongated bodies and well-forked tail. However, there are tradeoffs. They are "pursuit' fish and can swim very fast to overtake their prey. But they cannot turn corners sharply, so prey will survive if it sees the pike coming and has learned to dart at right angles to cover. Pike are toothy critters. This tells you that they are "grabbers." They must grab and stun the prey, release it and turn it head first into their mouths. This is true of many species, in that bait fish can only be swallowed head first. I learned years ago in Canada trolling with minnows for lake trout, to not set the hook on the first hit, as the laker will come back and swallow the stunned minnow head first.

Let us examine the popular largemouth bass from a form standpoint. They are the "full backs" of the sports fish, and the old females develop large stomachs, particularly pre-spawn. Lunkers

Clarence Kalkofen.
Northern pike.

21

hide and ambush their prey. They are built for short yardage spurts, so their body is formed accordingly. They have large mouths and "slurp" in their prey. They engulf their prey by flaring their gills while passing water through them, literally sucking the prey into their cavernous mouth. Using the word "bite" relative to a largemouth is not accurate. Their teeth have almost all disappeared from lack of utility, and that is why you can lift them by the lower lip (not recommended, nor is flipping them into the bottom of a boat for that matter). Largemouth bass are "shoal" fish and "school" primarily when juvenile to corral baitfish, like shad, in open water.

Red drums are a great, strong coastal fish. They eat shrimp, crabs, mollusks and small fish, so they are essentially toothless. They travel in schools. In the same ecology is seatrout (weakfish), but seatrout have teeth as they primarily catch baitfish and shrimp to eat.

Fish in the sunfish family are not built for speed, as it is not needed for feeding. They feed on insects, small fish and crustaceans. Their ecology is where their food base exists, and there is no need for a toothy mouth structure. Their strategy for survival and feeding is their camouflage amongst debris, fallen trees and other such detritus.

Referring to Illustration 1, most fresh water fish have the upper half of their body a very dark color, while their bellies have white pigmented scales. This is the normal counter shading of fishes. This shading lowers the contrast of the fish from the viewing background, when a predator is above the fish. When the predator is viewing from below it cannot see the prey's under belly against the overhead sky. Some fish like Stripers and White Bass have a series of horizontal stripes. When we get to Chapter Five, Lure Decoration, we will get into the details of prey and predator camouflaging patterns, and how it should be considered relative to lure designs.

What cannot be shown is that fish are cold blooded creatures like frogs and snakes and their activity levels are controlled directly by the temperature of the water in which they live. We will discuss this later in Chapter Four, when we cover the subject of brightness. We will demonstrate why the thermometer is a fisherman's best friend, and not solely for the realm of fly-fishermen who are into etymology.

Sensory perception

Illustration 1 also shows the body and head lateral line receptors and also, the location of the smell and taste receptors, and eyes.

Fishes' eyes are generally similar to humans' with major exceptions. Fish do not have eyelids nor do their pupils expand and contract. Humans can modulate light intensity automatically with their pupils and eye lids if necessary. Beyond that they can wear sunglasses. Fish must modulate brightness by vertical and horizontal columns of water, which vary in color (clear water is actually blue, as in clear blue). A lot more about this later, as controlling the brightness of a lure is a critical consideration.

The majority of our game fish can see color quite well. Most fish have two sets of rods and cones in their retina, while humans have three. But they can distinguish color adequately, and in some case their sight becomes specialized for certain prevailing water conditions. For example, a salmon's eyes are blue and green sensitive while in the ocean and become red sensitive when they enter fresh water to seek a mate and spawn. Toward evening fishes' eyes begin adapting to diminishing light conditions and change to night vision, seeing shades of gray and black well.

Fish can see color, but there are no colors that fish prefer over another. They are not intelligent animals. "Hot colors" only exist in the fisherman's mind. A particular "hot color" is only one that fits a particular fishing situation, usually when conditions are stable. When the fishing conditions change, the hot lures become "cold turkeys." It has nothing to do with any color preferences of fish. In fact, when a particular color lure is overused (like in tournaments) we will see that fish can be "turned off." So, when you hear about a "hot color," save your money and do not rush to the nearest tackle shop.

The hearing senses of fish reside in two areas: the two inner ears with enclosed chambers on each side of the skull (which maintain a fish's equilibrium as well) and the lateral line, which plays an important role in the acoustical system.

The inner ear can hear a broad spectrum of sound frequencies dependent upon the species, but 30 to 3000 Hz is normal. Their hearing is biased to the lower frequencies (for a good reason), and does not have the broad frequency range of humans. Humans are fortunate that they have ears on both sides of their heads, because we can tell from which direction the sound is coming. Not so with fishes, as the inner ears are very close together and sound arrives at them almost simultaneously. I know of no species that uses sound as the primary predation mechanism. Fish can be stimulated by sound to a state of alertness, but must focus on the prey with sight. Fish are attuned to the lower "natural baitfish frequencies," because of the low frequency generated by the tail of the prey while it is swimming. Yet today's fishermen are caught up with all sorts of lures with "rattles," assuming that the rattling sound attracts the fish. I know of no legitimate statistical study that suggests that rattles improve the performance of a lure. Fish can filter out extraneous frequencies and focus on the ones to which they are conditioned. Rattles send out lots of harmonic high frequencies. I doubt if they mean anything to the fish. Sound must emulate the noises that prey and predator transmit to be of any worth.

The lateral line system is a fascinating sensory complex. No need to get into a technical description of how the lateral lines work. Suffice it to say that it is a string and grouping of sense organs, called neuromasts, exposed to water through pores and connecting ducts. "Being able to perceive water flow and minute changes in its speed has many useful applications for fish. Because of the lateral line system, fish can feel the presence of nearby objects, can synchronize its swimming motion with that of other fishes in a school, can detect the direction of running water and maintain position within it, can communicate with other fish, and can perceive surface waves produced by struggling insects that have fallen in the water."[2] Experiments have found that the lateral lines serve to detect low frequency vibrations.[3] Also, there is convincing evidence that predatory fish use their lateral line system to detect prey[4] and vice versa. Some shoal fishes can communicate with grunts, groans and bone grinding too. All in all, the hearing senses of fish are quite remarkable.

Now let's examine olfaction, the act of smelling. Paul Johnson's *The Scientific Angler* does a fine job of covering this topic from a fisherman's standpoint.[5] He spends a great deal of time on smell tracks, the positive, neutral and negative chemical tracks that impact a fish's behavior. Well worth the read for the serious fisherman. It is out of print now, but used copies may be obtainable on www.abebook.com.

There are endorsements and skepticism about fish scents relative to bait enhancement and scented plastic lures. There are a lot of "magic potions and juices" in the marketplace with mostly unfounded claims. So, let's see what research tells us.

In *Bass West Magazine*, Berkley scientist Dr. Keith Jones writes: "So if bass have such a good sense of smell, why can't they follow odor trails? What stops them from smelling their way to your scent-enhanced lure? The answer lies in the physics of chemical dispersions and in the way that most fish noses are externally structured.

"In a nutshell, odors emanating from an object in water do not produce smooth concentration gradients. Instead, the odor distributions tend to be discontinuous and patchy. Turbulence in the water produces small clouds or swirls that yield high concentrations of the odor surrounded by neighboring waters with virtually no odor at all. A bass moving through such a patchwork odor field would be faced by a jumbled array of sensory information having no rhyme or reason. One minute it would be smelling a hefty dose of the scent, the next it would be sniffing empty space." The exception to this is where the fish and scented bait are in very close quarters. Also, scents can be tracked in current by fish, and detected when a bait is moving down current over them. Jones goes on to say that scent can "alert" bass to the presence of prey, and change their "attitude." Well, there are two facts that would suggest otherwise. Bass are visual predators and are not conditioned (see Chapter Two, Fish Behavior) to utilizing smell when foraging for prey. Secondly, he says "fish scents dramatically alter a bass's 'attitude.'" Intelligent humans have attitudes, not fish (as we address in Chapter Two). Technically, fish can be stimulated to behave in an alert manner.

The olfactory nares, shown in Illustration 1, are located close together on the frontal part of the head, too close to allow most fish to discern the direction from which the smell is coming. It is a different story with some catfish who use scent to locate prey—their nares are wide

Jennifer Kirk. Brookie.

apart. There is no doubt that the sense of smell in fishes is relatively acute as proven in many experiments. It is estimated that a fish's smell is one million times better than human's. Salmon are a prime example, as they return upstream to the spawning ground where they became smolts, and where the chemistry of the water was imprinted upon them.

There are mechanical problems with scented plastic lures. Topical scent washes off very quickly, and scent captured inside the plastisol of which the lure is made cannot escape. Plastisol is not soluble in water. Only Exude™ brands plastic baits from Mister Twister™ really work properly. They have a patented formulation wherein the plastisol is water soluble and the scent sloughs off continuously.

Some species rely on olfaction, others use their sense of taste, and some exploit both. It is often necessary to lump olfaction and taste together in any discussion of the effect of odor on fish, by utilizing the term chemoreception. But olfaction is distinct anatomically from the sense of taste, which is based on taste buds located in the mouth, and often on the body itself, as with some catfish.

Chemoreception is utilized in several unique ways in fish. When a prey fish is injured, for example by a pike, it gives off a chemical alarm substance, which warns its shoal mates. They actually smell danger. But it also warns other pike that prey are in distress and they come to get their share. Alarm systems are but one example how olfaction can be used by fish to communicate.

Another is the attraction of the opposite sex. In a great number of species, females that have ovulated release a fluid from their ovaries. The effect on the males is as you would expect; they begin an active search for the female, and increase their courtship behavior, nest building and aggression toward other males. When female salmon lay their eggs, the male produces milt and also presses the female to release more eggs.

The ordinary smell of skin mucus can help fish identify others of the same species. Many experiments have been conducted on salmon, catfish, carp, and others. Each time, good evidence for olfactory detection of conspecifics was obtained.

Thus, while fish are not brainy or intelligent, they have unbelievable sensory perceptions to compensate and hence ensure their survival.

Analyzing fish in human terms causes all sorts of problems. Fish do not have the brain capacity to think or act intelligently. How many times have you heard words such as "like," "smart," "sulking," "attitude," "prefer," or similar used to describe a fish's actions? Not only do they not apply, they preclude us from really understanding why fish do what they do.

There is no such thing as intelligence. We say a person is intelligent, but what we mean is that the person acts intelligently.[7] Almost all of our intelligent acts involve language, either in our reading, speaking, or thinking. Many of our acts are intelligent, but people also react to many events (stimuli) without giving thought to their reactions. Note how sometimes when you are washing your hands you get a call to nature—a classic Pavlovian response. This kind of response is called a *conditioned response*. Animals do not think or act intelligently, they just behave, which distinguishes animals from man.

All complex acts are learned through the process of *stimulus-response-reinforcement*. *Reinforcement* can be positive or negative. If the reinforcement is positive and repeated soon and often after the response, the behavior will likely be repeated. This process is called *conditioning* or *learned behavior*. When a *response* is punished, that behavior is unlikely to be repeated, at least in the near term. In many cases in the fish world, the wrong behavior is punished with death, as they fall prey to their predators. Fish species survive this process because many thousands of eggs are spawned, and enough fish learn appropriate responses to reach maturity—thus ensuring the species' survival. *Learned behavior* also allows fish to adapt to a changing ecology.

So if a fish's behavior is essentially "learned," how can they survive very long after birth without inherited survival instincts? Well, it goes like this: creatures (fish) do not inherit large amounts of needed response patterns, but they inherit the capacity to be reinforced by certain events, for example, the capacity to imprint on their parents. They inherit the ability to learn.[8] While it may not be technically correct, some people would refer to this as "inherited instinct."

To become a better fisherman, we must learn what *conditioning* is all about, as it plays a major role in how fish behave. If a fish does not *learn* through *conditioning* to respond properly to the many daily stimuli, they do not live long. Adult fish have learned a repertoire of many appropriate responses. In fact, lunker fish have adapted specific behaviors that their brethren have not, and grow to a ripe old age. They behave differently, and if we wish to catch lunker fish we must fish for them differently than we would their shoal mates. That is why tournament fishermen go for numbers instead of pursuing one or two large fish, as lunkers are far more difficult to catch since they behave differently.

My son and I flyfish the San Juan River in New Mexico periodically. It is an all-year fishery since the water flows out from beneath the Navajo Dam. The river contains lots of grass in which very small midge nymphs abound, and of course the rainbows are *conditioned* to the abundance of these small nymphs. The operant "fly" is a size 26 midge and fished on a 2X tippet. The large rainbows are in slots where the nymphs flow by, and have to move barely an inch to suck in their food. The minimum size fish you can keep is twenty inches, which is not a problem, as the vast majority of fly-fishermen smartly fish catch and release. This is classic *conditioning*, in the insect feeding trout world. Of course, when the rainbows are not gorging on specific foods, or food is scarce, they will hit lures.

One day, while I lived in Austin, Texas, Ralph Mann called me. Ralph is a researcher/writer for *In-Fisherman*. He said, "Phil, let's go to Burnet Lake tomorrow, there is a heck of a "trap" bite on." Ralph had fished the lake many times, and knew all the good structure. And of course, we had our "trap" lures rigged and ready. To make a long story short, we did not get a hit all morning on our "trap" lures. Why? Because there had been a tournament the day before, and the bass had become *conditioned* to avoid the rattling "trap" lures by being caught, stung and released. We rescued the day by fishing some structure around seventeen feet deep and jigging Mepps Syclops™ spoons on a batch of fish that apparently had not been *negatively conditioned* during the prior day's tournament. So stay clear of a tournament lake for several days or try to figure out which lures have not "stung" the fish.

While in Austin, I built my custom rods at the Rodmaker's. There was always a video tape about fishing on the TV. One popular tape was taken in Florida, where they would ring a bell, on the dock, near the surface of the water every day at the same time. Then they would dangle a big night crawler near the surface, and a very large bass would come up and slurp it down. I have seen several other tapes that show how fish are *conditioned* in this manner. In this case the behavior psychologist calls it *operant conditioning*, as an operator controls the reinforcement. This is classical conditioning.

So, we are mistaken to suggest that fish act intelligently. They are simple animals with an extraordinary sensory system that lets them learn behaviors that allow them to survive.

Biting-reacting-reflex striking

To use the term "bite" is a misnomer when it comes to fishing. I am afraid we are stuck with the term "bite", so let's use it knowing that is a general term for fish activated action at the end of the line. It is common to hear the term that fish are "on the bite," when active, whether it be from foraging or a reactive strike.

Fish "bite" lures for several reasons. They forage to satiate hunger, or react (conditioned response) to other stimuli. If we wait for fish to be hungry to "bite" we wait a long time between action.

When anadromous fish enter rivers to spawn, they cease eating, but readily strike lures. When bass are on the spawning beds, they are not eating and are very aggressive. These are "reflex" strikes which are responses resulting from life long conditioning.

From a behavioral viewpoint we are trying to stimulate a fish to action. Another word for stimulation is "trigger," and we as fishermen are always trying to "trigger" a fish to "biting."

When fish are in a neutral state, not foraging, the trick is to generate a stimulus which will cause the fish to attack the lure. They are not hungry, but are conditioned to react to certain stimulus. These conditioned reactions are true of people as well as animals.

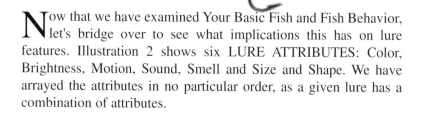

Now that we have examined Your Basic Fish and Fish Behavior, let's bridge over to see what implications this has on lure features. Illustration 2 shows six LURE ATTRIBUTES: Color, Brightness, Motion, Sound, Smell and Size and Shape. We have arrayed the attributes in no particular order, as a given lure has a combination of attributes.

Color and brightness

Let's examine Color and Brightness first, since seeing the prey is critical to most fishes' feeding success. In the final analysis, the lure

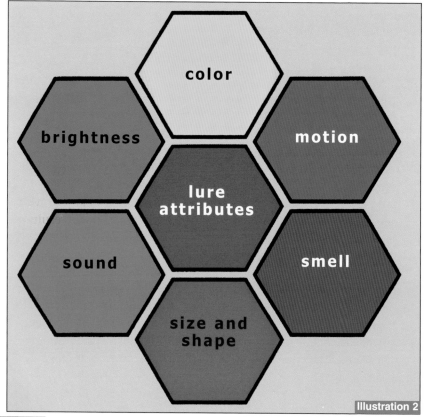

Illustration 2

must be seen to be engulfed. Most predator fish forage by sight. In an experiment, Dr. Loren G. Hill "found that fish use sight almost 100% in their selection of food. Yes, they are influenced by sound, smell, texture and taste, but sight is their dominant sense by far. How did we determine this? We put translucent caps over the eyes of the fish and found that they could only find natural food (crawfish) in six percent of the times offered. But take the caps off and plug their olfactory openings so they could not smell the food, and they found the food every time. It became obvious that the fish may know that food is nearby, through any of their senses, but if they can't see it they have a hard time getting it."[9]

Fish are not "attracted to" or "prefer" any particular color. A lure's color is important only as it makes the lure visible against the background upon which the fish is viewing it. A particular color helps fish see the lure, under specific water conditions, light conditions and fishing depth. We go into this in great detail in Chapter Four, Color Technology. We will see that the color that fishermen see in daylight is not the color that fish see in the water. Selecting the right lure color is critical to selecting a high odds lure. Knowing how to choose the right lure color is an area where the vast majority of fishermen can markedly improve their catch rate.

Brightness is a part of the color equation. Some colors are brighter than others, and some metal plates are brighter than others. Because fish are cold-blooded, the amount of light a fish can tolerate is dependent upon the water's temperature. The colder the water, the brighter a lure needs to be to stimulate fish to action. As the water temperature rises during late spring and summer, we must use less bright lures. When a lure is too bright for a fish, the rods and cones in the retina are overloaded, not unlike a person looking into bright light or driving into the sun. As noted earlier, fish can modulate overall sunlight by controlling their depth or seeking shade. But if a lure is too bright, they will back away or "spook" from it. When they back away from a lure, they put a column of colored water between their eyes and the lure, like putting on colored glasses.

My first encounter with lure brightness was on a backpacking trip in Canada in the early 60s. We were hiking up an old abandoned logging road to a lake. On the way, the road crossed a small stream where there was a series of active beaver ponds. The ponds were shallow, with silted bottoms. You could see the native brookies hanging around. This was before spinning rods and open face reels were popular, and we had enclosed, side mounted, model 80 Johnson™ spinning reels that were designed to use on a fly rod. So, with one rod we could fly or spin fish. One of our favorite lures was a small Acme Phoebe™ spoon. We had both silver and gold plated ones. We caught plenty of brookies, but only on the gold plated Phoebe. It was not long before we were fighting over the only gold one left. It was not until many years later that I figured it all out. Because the water was relatively warm, and the sun was out, the silver spoon was too bright and spooked the fish. Just by "toning down" to gold, we caught plenty of fish.

A couple of summers ago in Alaska we were fishing for sea-run cutthroats. It had not rained for a long time and the water in the stream was very low and warm. One of my friends caught no fish as he stubbornly stuck with his favorite silver bladed spinner. I soon toned down to a Mepps tarnished brass See Best™ spinner and caught fish, cast after cast. My son was using a wooly bugger on his fly rod and did well too.

Much of my early spinner development and testing for Mepps was conducted in Colorado when we summered for six weeks to escape the Texas heat. In August and early September the Colorado streams are low and relatively warm due to all the draw downs from irrigation. I spent two summers testing the Mepps XD™, and found out that anything with a fluorescent red bead was too bright for warmer water and the bright summer skies. Under these conditions, you could see the fish follow the fluorescent, red beaded, XD up from the bottom, but as they got near the surface the lure became too bright and they spooked off. Once I started using a black XD, I caught plenty of fish. So brightness is a very important part of the color selection process.

Steelheaders use a lure called a ""yarn ball," which is no more than colored yarn connected to the hook with a "sliding bait loop" Colors are mixed: fluorescent pink, green, chartreuse, and others like nothing in nature. Aside from drifting, the only attribute is color.

Motion

Next let's examine the Motion attribute. The first thing a juvenile fish sees after it spawns is motion-particularly the motion of their parents around the nest. From day one, motion is a prime stimulus for fish. Naturally, they have to see the lure to be stimulated by motion. But a lure that looks nothing like prey, if it generates the right stimulating motion, catches lots of fish. Remember too, that fish have their natural camouflage, and prey are hard to see unless they are in motion.

Tom Seward designs outstanding crankbaits for the Yakima Bait Co. We have known each other for years. I design spinners, and he designs exceptional crankbaits. One real treat is to hear him lecture on how to fish crankbaits. In one of the many articles he wrote for Fishing Facts magazine, he says "your favorite imitation may really not be perceived by a bass as you see it, and often another similar lure would have done just as well. Big bass are most interested in lures that imitate vulnerability and distress, rather than lures that imitate specific prey."[10]

Most bass fishermen have witnessed this kind of an event. You cast a spinnerbait to a submerged outcropping. And while the bait is descending and just before it hits the water, an eruption occurs, with the bass inhaling your spinnerbait. This has happened so many times that it is almost a routine thing. So, strike one up for motion, as the bass has no time to detect anything else.

Sound

It seems nowadays that every bait must rattle-this is nonsense. Do not buy into that hype, the boys are putting the shuck on you. Fish are attuned to the natural sounds prey make. Fish are "conditioned" to particular sounds. Other arbitrary sounds are meaningless and essentially filtered out. In other words, fish selectively learn the "good sounds" that exist in their ecology.

There are two basic natural sounds: low frequency sounds that are generated when the prey is swimming, and distress sounds when one of their fellow prey are in trouble. We mentioned in Chapter Two the role of lateral lines, which hear low frequency sounds and are used for foraging.

"Nothing can trigger a response in a fish faster that the vibrations set up by an injured fish. The sounds produced by a wounded fish are totally different from those created when a fish is swimming normally. Beyond any doubt, predatory fish are attracted by vibrations given off by another fish in distress"[11]. Mepps Aglia™ spinners have been around for three generations because of the low frequency vibrations generated, plus their ability to emulate wounded prey.

The better crankbaits are a close second in that they can imitate the sound of prey. The balsa wood Rapala™ has been around for years too, and until recently had no rattles, but they bowed to the fisherman's follies and Rapalas now have them in many lures. I wonder how we ever caught fish over the years without rattles? Arbitrary noise makers like rattles, vibration chambers, clackers and so on mean nothing to a preying fish, and in many cases can produce negative results, as noted.

Smell

To make a pun, "this is a real can of worms." There are things that lures that "smell" can do and things they cannot do. Live bait is obviously a smelly bait, but is the predator keying on smell, sound or visual cues? We know that a majority of fish are sight feeders, but can a lure that smells improve its odds? We mentioned "smell tracks" earlier, and the inability of fish to directionally hone in on scented lures. But, when a fish gets a whiff of a scent to which it is positively conditioned, it can be stimulated to a state of alertness, and it can forage around until its visual acuity takes over. Most fish scents are some form of natural bait extraction or, in plastic baits, some form of amino acid.

From a scented lure standpoint, the most popular ones are plastic baits, made of a polyvinyl chloride (PVC) called plastisol. The problem with PVC is that it is not water soluble and any scent that is in the plastisol is trapped, and cannot escape, or is topical and washes off quickly, and here again the fisherman has been conned into believing the marketing hype. There now is one scented plastic bait, that is recent to the marketplace, that really works. It is Exude™, by Mister Twister™. In this formulation, the PVC becomes soluble at the water interface and the scent continually sloughs off. I was skeptical at first. But I have seen so much convincing evidence that Exude™ really works, that I now use Exude™ when fishing plastics.

Dave Pitts. Steelhead.

Size and shape

How many of you have caught big fish on small lures, or small fish on big lures-most everyone. These are reactive strikes. In general, fish are efficient animals and eat accordingly. Small fish take prey that is 40 to 50 percent of their own length, and full-grown predators tend to favor prey that is 10 to 20 percent of their own length. A 30 inch pike's average prey is around 9½ inches. Large fish have conditioned themselves to take prey that is commensurate with their esophagus. If not, the prey would probably get stuck half way down.[12]

So there is validity to the saying "large baits for large fish." As your baits get larger, however, you must be careful that they are not too bright. At Lake Fork in Texas (where a number of state record fish have been caught) they use large crankbaits and large live bait to go after double digit bass. In the reservoirs in California, they use large rainbow trout imitators since these world record bass forage on adult rainbow trout. This is not to say that large fish do not eat smaller bait that may be plentiful, and prey that are in distress are particularly vulnerable.

I have seen no studies on the shape of lures. Taxidermists find a great variety of prey and other objects in the stomachs of large bass. Fish are opportunistic feeders, and eat about anything that is handy. It is conceivable that if a particular prey was dominant in a predator's habitat, a fish could be conditioned to a particular shape. My guess is that other lure attributes are much more important. Fly-fishermen key on fish that are conditioned to the predominant insect in the water, and here I think size and shape of the fly or nymph are important.

Back in the sixties, I read stories in Fishing Facts magazine written by Buck Perry, the father of structure fishing. He told stories of how he would win bets by catching bass on arbitrary pieces of wood on which he attached hooks.

The Mepps™ spinner looks like nothing in Mother Nature, and is "The World's #1 Lure." So much for the importance of a lure's shape.

Kay Lynn Butterfield. Northern Pike.

If I had to choose one lure attribute as principal, it would be Color. The large majority of predators are sight feeders, and in the end, must see the prey to engulf it. There are four elements of color technology: contrast, color, brightness and water temperature.

Contrast

Fish view their prey against a background. If there is little or no contrast between the lure and the background upon which it is viewed, a fish cannot effectively pursue it. Camouflaged prey survive because there is no contrast between themselves and their background. We do not want our lures to survive! Fish view prey against many backgrounds—for example, open water, a horizontal column of water, the bottom, the sky overhead, natural vegetation, rocks and so on. In open water, the water's color changes with depth. Light can penetrate near the surface, depending upon the water's clarity, and here the water is light in color, but as you go deeper, the water becomes darker and more and more monochromatic. Instead of direct sunlight, the light bounces off the particles in the water and becomes indirect light. This indirect light can perhaps be better understood if you picture it as "colored fog." Sunny, cloudy or shady conditions make a big difference in the background color. Also, the water's color creates a backdrop against which the lure is viewed. It is axiomatic then to use dark lures against a light background and light hues against a dark background. The opposite of what fishermen have been taught.

Color

Fish can see some colors better than others, but they have no hankering for a particular color. Fish's eyes can be more sensitive to particular colors, depending upon the ecology in which the fish lives.[13] Salmon's eyes are blue and green sensitive when in the ocean, but become red sensitive during spawning. Walleyes have eye structures that allow them to see shades of gray, brown and black to accommodate their ecology. Bass and many other fish have

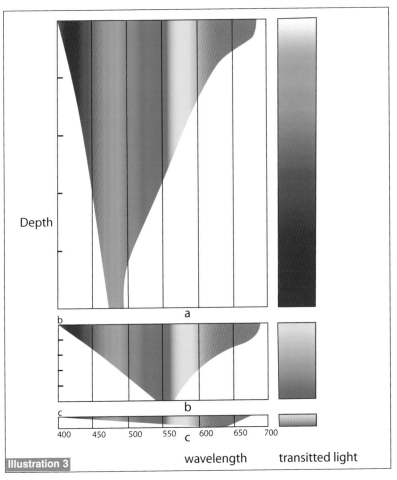

Depth

b

c

400   450   500   550   600   650   700

Illustration 3   wavelength   transitted light

excellent night vision which discerns the dark shades of night, and their eyes begin adapting to night vision during twilight.

We classify a water's color in three categories: Blue, Green and Turbid. Remember sunlight contains all the colors of the rainbow.

Clear Blue water transmits primarily blue wavelengths due to water's molecular structure. The sky is blue for the same reason. As light penetrates glaciers, you probably have noted the bottom of the glacier becomes bluish for the same reason.

Green water contains yellow-green phytoplankton and dissolved organic matter from plants and animals, and filters out all but green wavelength light.

Turbid water contains tannins and lignins and other products of more complete plant decomposition. This water passes light in the red part of the spectrum, and usually appears tea, dark or ruddy brown in color.

When light rays impact colored surfaces directly it is called "direct" light and the water shows a light hue. When the surface is illuminated by reflected lightrays, it is called indirect lighting and the surface color becomes darker.

Transmission of light by water is dependent on the color or the wavelength of the light.[14] Levine and MacNichol's work is seminal in the study of fish's eyes and how they see under water. In Illustration 3, we reexamine their findings relative to how wavelengths of light penetrate blue, green and turbid waters:

In clear oceans and lakes (a) the light becomes increasingly monochromatic and blue as depth increases.

In water that carries green organic matter (b) light at all wavelengths are absorbed more quickly than in clear water, and the light becomes dark green sooner.

In rivers, swamps and marshes that carry large amounts of the products of plant and animal decay, tannins and lignins, (c), absorption is rapid and the spectral distribution of the light shifts to the red. Note the relative depth of light penetration for each color, and how it changes with depth.

So if a red object (non fluorescent) is placed in a few feet of clear blue water, it cannot reflect red because the red wavelength is filtered out by the water and the objects show black. It is a misnomer, but sometimes this is called the "black shift." Any colored object that is placed in water where its wavelength of light does not exist will show dark, or the absence of color. This is why lures do not look the same in the water to the fish as they look to the fisherman in sunlight. And, if we are to have lures that contrast with the background upon which the fish views the lure, we must know the resulting color of the lure in different water colors and depths.

In Paul Johnson's *The Scientific Angler*, and Colin Kageyama's, *What Fish See*,[15] real underwater photographs are shown that illustrate many of the varieties of colors under water. Both Johnson and Kageyama have an interest in scuba diving. Colin, a colleague of mine, is a fishing optometrist and a first class steelhead fisherman. Colin and I teamed up to develop Mepps' See Best™ line of spinners.[16] This line of spinners has a "selection guide" that determines which spinner to use under specific conditions.

Instead of donning scuba gear, I have built an underwater simulator with special filters and varying light intensities, which we use in our research and development, and while decorating lures.

Brightness

We experience brightness in one form or other almost daily-when we go from a dark room into sunlight, when we drive into the sun and when a bright light shines in our eyes. We have noted that fish eyes do not dilate nor do they have eyelids. The rods and cones in their retinas can adjust to light in several hours, but generally speaking fish modulate bright sunlight by putting a column of water between themselves and the water's surface or a bright object (not unlike wearing sunglasses). They also readily seek shade or hide behind logs or rocks.

We say the sun is bright when we are bombarded by many photons of light. Colors reflect photons of light in the color's narrow band width. Fluorescent colors are even brighter than non-fluorescent colors.

Eyes can only absorb so many photons of light in a particular portion of the spectrum or they become overloaded. We cited several anecdotal stories earlier about brightness. But there is a little more to it than that. For example, if we are fishing in turbid water, on a bright day, with a fluorescent orange lure, the lure will appear tan as the fish's eyes are overloaded in the red spectrum. The water will appear tan too and the fish will not see the lure as there is no contrast between lure and background. A fish's sensitivity to light is dependent upon the water's temperature. They can tolerate very bright lures during the winter months when the water is cold and the sun at a low angle, but get "blinded" very easily in the summer when the water is warm.

While in Austin, Texas, I fished our golf course ponds every Monday when the course was closed. In the winter, with cold water, I would catch seven-pound bass on bright Mepps™ spinners. And the fish were shallow even on sunny days as their tolerance for brightness increased with the decreasing water temperature and low sun angles.

To illustrate this phenomenon, let's go fishing for silver salmon (Coho) in a river in Alaska. Silver salmon like to rest in slack pools,

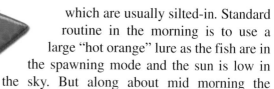

which are usually silted-in. Standard routine in the morning is to use a large "hot orange" lure as the fish are in the spawning mode and the sun is low in the sky. But along about mid morning the silvers that were biting so great are turned off-what happened? Well, we now have the aforementioned condition, and the lure is too bright. All you have to do is tone down the brightness by going to a darker lure, and like magic, the fish turn on again.

Water temperature

Why are we discussing water temperature in this chapter on Color Technology? Why, because fish are cold blooded and their tolerances and actions are determined by the temperature of the water in which they live. There is a theory that fish will have a "preferred temperature range." There are several considerations that tend to make this theory impracticable. Fish must have oxygen to live, and must therefore be in water with sufficient oxygen. Also, they must be near their forage, and they must control the brightness of the light impacting their eyes. In lakes, it is conceivable that they may seek optimum water temperatures, but I do not know how workable that is. They may have a chance in lakes to find a "preferred" water but in rivers it would be very limited. Of course, dams can modulate the

Exhibit 1
Range of Optimum (Cool) Temperatures

Species	Temperature Range
Atlantic Salmon	57-61
Pacific Salmon	53-55
Silver Salmon (Coho)	52-57
Steelhead	46-54
Rainbow Trout	51-59
Brown Trout	57-68
Brook Trout	53-65
Yellow Perch	60-70
Striped Bass	56-61
Largemouth Bass	68-75
Smallmouth Bass	65-71
Spotted Bass	74-76
Walleye	60-70
Rock Bass	59-70
Muskellunge	60-70
Northern Pike	50-70
Panfish	65-75
Lake Trout	45-55

water's temperature a lot, both upstream and downstream. Remember, a fish must first eat and survive, and seeking a "preferred" water temperature is probably not a priority.

I have caught huge pre-spawn rainbow trout in 34 degree water with bright Mepps See Best™ spinners. They were eating salmon smolt and sculpin. How do I know that? My son Mike caught them too on smolt and sculpin patterns on a fly rod.

One New Year's weekend on Toledo Bend in Texas, son Mike and I caught our limit of bass in one morning while it was snowing and the water was in the 40s. We had ten fish for a total of 46 pounds.

What do these two anecdotes tell you about the "preferred" temperature theory? Instead of "preferred" temperatures, it is more accurate to classify them as "optimum." You can catch lots of fish outside the "optimum" range.

We divide water into three ranges: Cold, Cool and Warm. When the water is Cold (colder than optimum), fish can tolerate bright lures, and it also requires brighter lures to stimulate them to action. When the water is Cold, fish are sluggish, their actions are slowed and they will not chase a lure very far nor very fast.

In the Cool (optimum) temperature range, fish are in their most active setting. They feed frequently, and will forage actively and with good efficiency. Total lure brightness should be in the mid-range.

When the water is Warm (warmer than optimum), we must tone down the lure's brightness substantially or the fish will spook or stand off. Because the sun is usually high, they seek cover or depth to modulate light intensity. They also become sluggish if it becomes very warm, as the warm water contains less oxygen. Darker and smaller lures are the order here.

Of course fly-fishermen carry thermometers to judge the insect cycles and hatches. But every fisherman should carry a thermometer, to determine how much brightness a particular species of fish can tolerate, or what it will take to stimulate them to action.

Exhibit 1 shows the Optimum (Cool) temperature ranges of many sports fish. When the temperature is below the Cool range the water is classified as Cold. When it is above the Cool range we classify the water as Warm.

So, remember the four elements of color technology: Contrast, Color, Brightness and Temperature. We will revisit these principles many times hereafter.

Plate 2a

Plate 2b

Non-fluorescent vs fluorescent color

Non-fluorescent colors look as intended under sunlight, but underwater they are substantially degraded. This happens because the non-fluorescent color reflects only a narrow wavelength band of color, and that wavelength must exist in the illuminating light for the color to be reflected. Fluorescent colors, on the other hand, can sustain their color and even reflect a brighter color. So, what is the difference between non-fluorescent and fluorescent colors?

Most fishermen believe that color fluoresces when it is bombarded by ultraviolet light. This is not totally true. A fluorescent color fluoresces when it is illuminated by light whose wavelength is shorter than its own. In other words, green light will fluoresce chartreuse, yellow, orange and longer wavelength colors like fluorescent red. Blue light will fluoresce all colors of longer wave lengths.

"Glow in the Dark" colors are luminescent, and will continue to glow a substantial time after the energizing light is absent. We will see later that "glow white" can be an effective color in certain water and light conditions.

Fluorescent colors range in brightness. In descending order they are chartreuse, pink, orange, green and blue. Of course, the area of color exposed on a lure determines brightness too.

When I give a talk on "lure selection and color technology," I like to start with my "red - blue water" exhibit. Here we have a blue background with variety of red lures attached. In the sunlight you see the exhibit and in Plate 2a, with all lures looking like they do in the tackle shop. But let us put them in clear Blue water, a few feet deep, as in Plate 2b. Note how some of the red lure decorations have turned black and some have not. The non-fluorescent lures have turned black, as non-fluorescent red must be exposed to the red wavelengths to reflect red. But the fluorescent red decorations maintain their color, because the blue lighted water has a shorter wavelength than red and energizes the fluorescent red pigment.

Now in Plate 2c, we put a blue filter between

Plate 2c

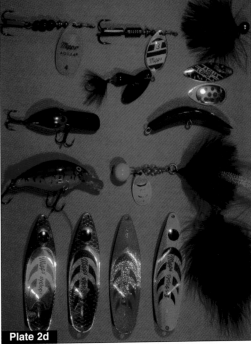

Plate 2d

Plate 2e

ourselves and the exhibit to simulate a column of blue water. This is just like wearing blue sunglasses, which filter out the red wavelength light and so the fluorescent reds appear black too.

Now let's look at the same lures in Green water, Plate 2d. Note the non-fluorescent reds show black, which is fine when it is sunny. The fluorescent reds show bright along with fluorescent chartreuse. Silver plate is great when, in direct light situations.

Now look at the same lures in Turbid water, Plate 2e, where all but red wavelengths are filtered out. Note how the reds "bleach" out due to overloading the rods and cones in the eyes of the fish. Reds are not appropriate for Turbid/Muddy water. the opposite to most fishermen's thinking.

What these plates tell you is that unless in shallow water, non-fluorescent red decorations appear black to the fish, while the fluorescent reds remain a bright red. Now if we view the lures from a distance, all the red decorations are black. So, fluorescent red is a "short distance color" and should be considered only in short range fishing circumstances. As we mentioned before, in the Colorado anecdote, if the fish is closing on a "black" lure and it turns "bright red" it will probably spook off. Red is probably the most misused lure color, and we must be cautious in its application or it does more harm than good. Fluorescent red is one is one of the "brightest" colors and should be treated as such. We will demonstrate where and when it should be used. Salmon fishermen are great users of red lures, in spawning runs, which is OK if the lure is not too "bright" for the conditions e.g. warmer turbid water. Fluorescent red shows a light tan in "turbid" waters, when the sun is overhead, and contrast is obviated.

Backgrounds

Fish can view lures against a variety of backgrounds. Near shore fish can view prey against the bottom, shoreline or many other objects. When looking outward from an ambush or in a large body of water, predators view their prey against a background determined by the clarity and color of the water, the viewing depth and whether it is sunny, overcast, raining or low light. Illustration 4 shows four shades of backgrounds, and how the color varies with depth and available sunlight. The actual colors vary, and are primarily determined by the water's clarity; then such things as light conditions and depth come into play. The term "colored fog" describes how the water's colors appear to the fish. In shallower water, color is determined a lot by whether that portion of the water is where direct light is penetrating, or is darker water where the light turns indirect (reflected from one particle of contamination to another). Most water is contaminated to varying degrees by particles in the

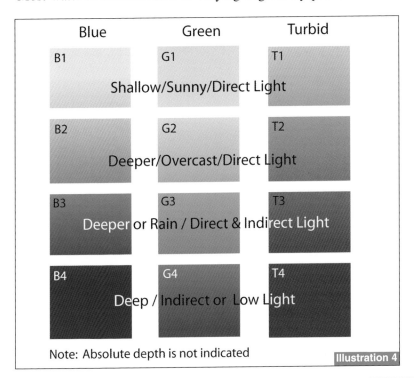

Blue	Green	Turbid
B1	G1	T1
Shallow/Sunny/Direct Light		
B2	G2	T2
Deeper/Overcast/Direct Light		
B3	G3	T3
Deeper or Rain / Direct & Indirect Light		
B4	G4	T4
Deep / Indirect or Low Light		

Note: Absolute depth is not indicated

Illustration 4

water. Our challenge is to pick a lure color that contrasts with the viewing background. Obviously, water clarity, depth and light intensity are all to be considered. Water can be a mixture of our basic Blue, Green and Turbid waters depending on the seasonal changes, e.g. snow melt, runoff, algae growth, roiling and other such factors. Light intensity varies with sun angle; overcast light intensity is 70% of direct sunlight, while drizzle is 50%.

To determine visibility (horizontal and vertical), lower a white drinking mug in the water and measure the depth at which it almost disappears, then double that distance. Beyond that point, the viewing background becomes dark rapidly. As seen in Illustration 4, absolute depth varies greatly for each basic water color, i.e. color B4 is roughly four times deeper than G4 and substantially deeper than T4.

Operative colors

The operative colors for Blue waters are white, fluorescent blue, fluorescent green, fluorescent chartreuse, silver plate and gold plate. For short range application, add fluorescent red, pink and fluorescent orange.

White provides good contrast only in clear water with direct light penetration. As you go deeper, white takes on the background color and contrast becomes limited. When you fish very deep, luminescent (glow white) is in order.

Both blue and green are great long distance colors, and those fish that live in the ocean or large bodies of water have eyes that are sensitive to blue and green. This is because the baitfish's underbelly takes on a blue or green cast.

Chartreuse is a fine universal blue water color. It can be seen from a long distance and is exceptional in deeper water.

Silver plate is outstanding in blue water where there is direct light. In indirect light, silver mirrors the water color and obviates contrast.

Gold plate is also outstanding in blue water, particularly when it is overcast. Gold plate is essentially a bright yellow color. But as you go deeper, you should switch to fluorescent chartreuse.

Fluorescent red, pink or orange are short range very bright colors, as noted, and should be restricted to when fish are in their spawning mode or cold water short range conditions.

For Green water, the operative colors are silver plate, fluorescent chartreuse, fluorescent red, orange or pink. Remember, a fish's vision is restricted in Green water, and we are only in the short range mode. In the direct light strata, a dark color like blue or black would be in order, particularly when the water warms.

In Turbid water, the operative colors are gold plate, fluorescent chartreuse and black. It is that simple. Remember too, that vision is extremely limited in very turbid water, and the fish will be shallow and near the shoreline.

In Texas many of the lakes have had their timber flooded, and their rotting makes the water "tea" colored. Anglers there fish for stripers and double digit bass with large, live, gold shiners. From our color technology, we know that "gold" is an operative color in turbid water. The gold fish contrast against the dark, tea-colored background. I told a colleague who fishes Lake Fork frequently that the best spinner bait would have gold blades and a black or black/chartreuse skirt in Lake Fork's turbid waters. The next time I saw him, he said that those colors were so effective that that is all he uses now.

In Low Light water conditions, Black, Glo White and Silver plate combine to make the applicable lure. Steelhead fisherman call this lure a "cop car." They are usually painted black and white to be seen at night and in low light conditions.

Metal lures

Spinners, spoons and blade baits have an advantage of other lures, in that they are made from brass and can be electroplated. A review of the relative brightness of metals, platings and finishes results in the following:

1. **Silver Plate**
2. **Gold Plate**
3. **Polished Brass**
4. **Polished Aluminum**
5. **Polished Copper**
6. **Chrome Plate**
7. **Nickel Plate**
8. **Tarnished Brass**
9. **Coffee**
10. **Black**

These variations in brightness give the lure designer great ability to design lures for various water temperatures and colors.

It may surprise the reader to know that chrome and nickel plates are not bright, and in cold water cannot be as effective those ranked at the top of the list. Until Mepps came along with the silver-plated Aglia™ spinner, most spinners had nickel blades, which are far less bright. That is one of many reasons why Mepps silver spinners are so effective in cold water.

Most spinner baits used by bass fishermen are nickel or chrome plate, which are inexpensive. But they cannot compare in effectiveness to silver in springtime *cold* water, and to gold in *turbid* water.

You might wonder about the brightness of silver and gold looking crankbaits. Well, crankbaits are sprayed with vaporized aluminum in a vacuum vessel. They are then coated with a clear or colored substrate. A crankbait cannot possibly be as effective in *cold* water as silver or gold plated brass since they are not nearly as bright. They are essentially *cool* and *warm* water baits. And that is why bass fishermen are successful with bright spinnerbaits in the spring when the water is *cold*.

George Martin. Bass.

Camouflaging

In order to decorate our lures so they are effective, we must be counter intuitive, and reject the common notion that lures must imitate the color and patterns of prey. We need to recognize that a predator must see its prey to pursue and engulf it. Camouflaging is a universal strategy for a prey's survival, plus a strategy of the predator so it is not seen by the prey.

In *Through the Fish's Eyes*,[17] Sosin and Clark in Illustration 5 show some basic camouflaging schemes and go on to say "Many species use color patterning for concealment. This type of camouflage is often called disruptive coloration because the pattern disrupts an observer's view of the fish. Because almost any camouflage system that breaks up the regularity of the body image will work..."

They discuss camouflaging in detail. "The most common camouflage pattern for concealment is 'countershading,' a gradual shading of the fish from dark on the upper surface to light underneath and across the belly. Look down on a body of water from above and it appears to be dark no matter how clear it really is. From

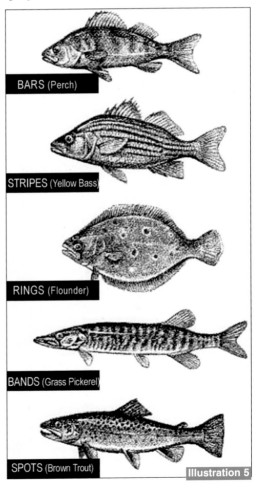

BARS (Perch)

STRIPES (Yellow Bass)

RINGS (Flounder)

BANDS (Grass Pickerel)

SPOTS (Brown Trout)

Illustration 5

the depths, however, the water appears bright against the sky. That is the reason for countershading and why practically every species of fish is dark on top and light on the bottom." Stripers have horizontal stripes, and when wave-induced, flickering light illuminates the stripes, disruptive camouflaging occurs.

They take note of fish that are silver sided beneath the dark upper surface. "But the silver sides would seem to be a poor defense. Actually, the silver pigment cells (called iridocytes) reflect the surrounding colors of the water and the bottom." This "reflective coloration" is "almost like hiding behind a mirror."

Ocean trollers have used "cut herring" as bait for many years, and it is just as popular today. The herring is cut at a compound angle, which causes the herring to roll. Hence, the term "herring roll." When the herring rolls, it eliminates the natural "counter shading," and obviates the herring's natural camouflage. It also creates a stimulating "wounded prey" action. They usually troll the herring behind a large "dodger" or "flasher" which is intended to be an attractor. But in fact, the dodger or flasher simulates another predator chasing the herring and other fish are stimulated to compete for the same herring. Also, ocean "trollers" and "moochers" will adorn their herring bait with colored "hoochie" (squid) skirts, or the Mister Twister Prop™. They claim it attracts the salmon, but in fact, it makes the herring contrast with the ocean background and counteracts the camouflaging. Color technology principles apply when selecting the color of hoochie skirts. In the ocean, green/fluorescent chartreuse skirts would be the most effective

The aforementioned Tom Seaward first designed crankbaits for the The Crankbait Co.™ years ago. Tom knew what he was doing and used countershading. The colors were reversed in that the lure was light on top and dark on the bottom. They were great lures, and I caught lots of fish on them. They soon disappeared from the market as no one was buying them since they thought they were painted incorrectly—little did they know.

All fish, whether predator or prey, have a natural camouflaging scheme. Yet lure manufacturers, in general, go out of their way to camouflage and make their lures lifelike, which makes no sense at all. As I said before, we do not want our lures to survive. Most of the lures I have relegated to the inactive bin are camouflaged, natural-

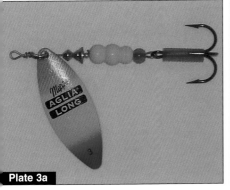

Plate 3a

Plate 3b

looking lures. Unless they have some kind of pigmentation that creates contrast under some water conditions, they are low odds lures.

Light on dark, dark on light

Thus, in lure decoration, we want the lure to contrast with the viewing background, and we want definition in our decorating. There is an axiom Colin Kageyama uses in lure decoration as well as in lure selection: "Light on Dark, Dark on Light" (LD-DL). In other words, a light-colored lure will contrast with a darker background and a dark lure with a lighter background. In decorating, you want LD-DL patterns. Again, lures that are decorated properly establish a pattern that produces contrast in themselves.

Blending

Care must be given that colors stay delineated, and the motion of the lure does not blend the colors together. This is particularly true of lures that have lots of motion. If the

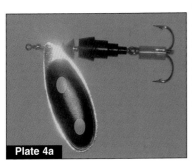

Plate 4a

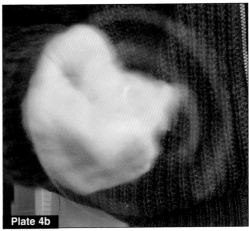

Plate 4b

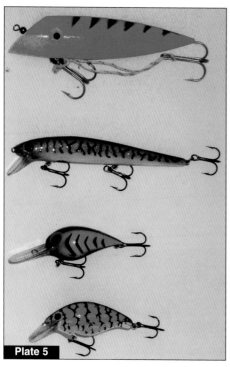

Plate 5

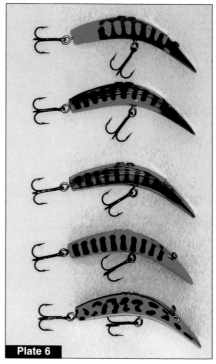

Plate 6

decorations align counter to the motion, you get color blending. The resulting color becomes a combination of the colors, with no delineation, and who knows what resulting color. So, lure decoration should compliment the dynamics of the lure, and the decoration should not be blurred by the action of the lure. Indeed, we will demonstrate how some lures utilize their motion to establish delineated patterns.

A couple of obvious perpetrators of color blending are the manufacturers and users of spinner blades, whether it be on spinnerbaits, inline spinners or spinner rigs. They decorate their blades radially, lengthwise on the blade. The blades look "fishy" and catch fishermen, but what color do the fish see when the blade is spinning, and how does it contrast against a given background?

Plates 3a and 3b show a Mepps "fire tiger" Aglia Long™ spinner decorated correctly and also functioning so you can see the color definition. Plates 4a and 4b show how the fish see the blade colors from behind a See Best™ spinner.

Chevrons and ladders

One of the better decorations to put on a lure is a "chevron" or "ladder" pattern, whether it is used on a spoon, plug, crankbait or topwater lure.

Plate 5 shows lures with a chevron pattern and two with a "naturalized" chevron treatment. All have excellent decoration schemes.

Plate 6 shows the venerable Flatfish™ with appropriate decorations.

Plate 7a and 7b is the author's popular Top Prop™ by Mister Twister™. It is a versatile, "stop and go," weedless, floating, topwater impeller bait. It is shown in the static mode, as well as in its "spinning" mode. The fish see this bait upwards on the surface. Note the dark circular rings that are generated and provide outstanding contrast against the sky.

In *VIEWING FISH In Their Own Realm*[18], Choronzey says "Cut plugs are hot items on the Great Lakes and with the aid of the camera I discovered day-in, day-out, blue, green or black, ladder backed, J-Plugs™ or Lymans™ produced best under all conditions and all depths." Note the mention of blue and green; two basic long distance colors to which salmon's eyes are sensitive.

Plate 8 shows a series of Mepps Syclops™ spoons, all of which have chevron decoration. And each has application to specific water and light conditions. Remember, it is preferable that lures be seen appropriately from all sides: top, bottom, front and rear.

When crankbaits are a solid color, they look the same from all sides. Typically they would be white, green, blue, black or chartreuse. Decorated LD-DL, these are very effective baits for given

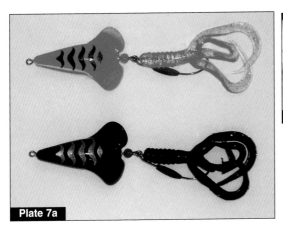

Plate 7a

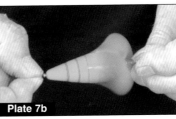

Plate 7b

water conditions (indirect lighting for example) as they can be viewed properly from all sides. I doctor most of my crankbaits by spraying the bottoms with a stripe of black paint, which eliminates any countershading so they can be viewed from below and behind much better.

Stroboscopic effect

Spinners, spoons and flashers have a feature that makes them very effective. Spinner blades can be decorated on both sides, and have a body color that contrasts with the back side of the blade. As the blade rotates around the body, you get a "stroboscopic" effect as the blade passes behind the body. This effect follows our LD-DL principle.

Spoons that have different colors or plating on each side exhibit the same principle as the spoon rotates or tumbles on the retrieve. Flashers differ from dodgers in that they rotate on the troll, and are therefore more effective. One side of the flasher should be a different color or plating than the other to provide the stroboscopic effect.

Tapes and pigmentation

The use of tapes is tricky and most users of tapes do not know what they end up with when the lure is underwater in various conditions. Most fishermen add tapes to enhance the lure, but have no idea what is accomplished. It may be good, but more likely would not provide needed contrast.

I have put many reflective tapes in my underwater simulator, and what you see in the daylight is not necessarily what is seen by the fish underwater. Your plain fluorescent tapes are OK, but be careful of the rest. Reflective tapes are essentially aluminum foil, some laser etched, and covered with a transparent colored substrate. What you end up with depends upon the pigment in the substrate, and who knows what the manufacturer uses. Looking good to the fisherman is no criterion for tape selection. "Silver" etched tapes reflect 25% less light than genuine silver plate, and therefore are not well suited for cold water application. Plus, they reflects the ambient water color and diminishes contrast.

The fly-fisherman who ties or buys exotic streamers for salmon and steelhead uses all sorts of dyed feathers, furs and yarns. Some materials do not readily absorb dyes well at all (particularly rabbit fur), and not all dyes are the same. What you get depends on the dye lots, too. Some yarns looks bright or fluorescent, but put them in a simulator and you will be surprised as to how the "fly" looks under water. You can buy a half dozen salmon flies from the same tier or dealer, but that is no guarantee that they are really the same under water, because the materials may be from different sources or dye lots, even though they look the same. Some fluoresce, some do not.

Howard Jennings.
Chinook.

Plate 8

6 Color revisited

Rivers

B efore we move on to succeeding chapters, let's apply the four elements of color technology: contrast, color, brightness and water temperature. Let's assume we are going to a small river with which we are not familiar, or have not fished for awhile. What is the first thing we should do? No, do not call the closest tackle shop near the location, or your buddy who has fished it recently and ask "what lures are hot?" Why? Because conditions can change overnight, and once we have gathered some basic information we can best sort it all for ourselves. And remember, for water that is heavily fished, the fish can be conditioned to avoid lures on which they have been caught and released. So, let's do our homework.

First of all, we know whether it is spring, summer, fall or winter, so we have a general idea of what the water temperature will be. But the first thing we need to do when we get there is check the water temperature, as that keys the whole process. We need to know the temperature range of the water: *cold*, *cool* or *warm*. Next, is the water *blue*, *green* or *turbid*? The river may be green from snow melt, or fed by a glacier, in which case it then would be *cold* too.

The river may be *turbid*, like the tea-colored rivers in the Upper Peninsula of Michigan, where the rivers drain cedar swamps. Or muddy due to rainy weather or dam release. If it is from a dam release, the water temperature can vary substantially from flood control or power generation demand. Water released from below a high dam can be colder than anticipated, independent of the time of year.

For the sake of brevity, I will be making this application with spinners as these are an outstanding and popular river lure.

Blue water

If the water is *cold*, we will need large, bright lures. If it is overcast, we will use silver-plated blades and bodies and fluorescent red decorations. If it is sunny, we will use silver-plated blades and brass bodies with fluorescent green decorations. If you have low light conditions, you will use combinations of silver-plated blades, black bodies and luminescent white decoration. These combinations stay the same for all other water temperatures too—only the size changes.

So how large is large? For example, in the case of spinners, for salmon it would be a #5, for a steelhead #4, for large trout or smallmouth it would be a #3 and for smaller fish #2. If you do not get a strike in a short time, start toning down the spinner's brightness by going a size smaller.

If the water is *cool*, we will need less bright spinners. This is achieved by reducing the spinner's size by a number, plus toning down the spinner's components. If it is overcast, we will use gold plated blades and brass bodies with black and green decoration. If it is sunny, we will use black blades and brass bodies with chartreuse decoration. For low light conditions, we will use the same 'low light" configuration as *cold*. All spinners should be one size smaller than *cold*.

If the water is *warm* and overcast we will use tarnished brass blades and green bodies and decorations. If it is sunny, we will use coffee colored blades, black body and green decoration. For low light conditions we will use the same configuration. All spinners should be one size smaller than *cool*.

**Mark Plath.
Smallmouth Bass.**

Turbid water

The configuration for *turbid* water is the same for all temperatures. However, as above, the size is reduced as the water warms. If it is either overcast or sunny, use gold plate and black body with fluorescent chartreuse and/or black decoration.

Green water

If the water is *green* in a river it is probably from snow or glacial melting. Use combinations of silver, fluorescent red and fluorescent chartreuse.

The more you know about the river, before you leave, the fewer lures you will need to take along. If you know the range of the river's temperature, all you need is four lures to catch fish shortly after you hit the river. Remember we are controlling brightness as well as color to provide maximum contrast in river conditions that differ due to the change in water temperature and sky conditions.

In the real world there is only one spinner manufacturer that designs to *color technology* criteria, and that is Mepps.

Trolling

Now let's go trolling in a lake, inlet or ocean and use spoons, spinners and plugs while applying our *color technology* principles. We learned in fishing our typical river the basic approach to spinner selection. For lakes it is basically the same, but there is far more latitude in viewing distances and backgrounds, plus there is the direct and indirect light experienced in fishing various depths. In the river we were keeping our spinner in contact with the bottom. In lakes, fish can be at any depth because they modulate light intensity by changing depth, and baitfish (or bait) can be at various depths.

Lakes can be *cold*, *cool* and *warm* too. Alpine lakes in the Rockies are generally *cold* the year round and are *green* during snow melt, changing to *blue* until freeze over. Some lakes in the South get *warm* in the long hot summers, plus the sun can be very bright in states like Texas and New Mexico. Some lakes are tea-colored (*turbid*) is they are full of rotting trees, typical of the many reservoir lakes in Texas and lakes whose feeder streams travel through swampy areas of cedar or cypress. Rocky lakes are generally clear, some even gin clear which we will discuss later as a special situation. Some lakes up North develop algae blooms which turn the water green. Some of the Great Lakes have *green* water when there is turbulence along sandy shores. So, lakes tend to have more variables than rivers, but follow the same lure selection principles as rivers. In other words, take your thermometer along to lakes too.

Trolling is a great way of covering a lot of territory, particularly when the fish are scattered in large bodies of water. It is fundamental then, that our decorations be long distance colors. And, as noted earlier, fluorescent red colors should be selectively used—in short range situations and when the water is *cold*, or when the fish are staging for spawning runs.

As we fish at greater depths, light becomes indirect, and polished metal and white lures mirror the water's color, obviating contrast. The depth at which direct light ceases and indirect light begins depends upon the clarity of the water. In some lakes, like Crater Lake in Oregon (which is gin clear), it is very deep. If it is an Alaska glacial inlet, it can be relatively shallow. Around Vancouver Island in British Columbia they troll for salmon at depths to 200 feet, and you know that is indirect light. The same goes for fishing for halibut and ling cod at 175 feet in Alaska—you know that is indirect light. In the rockier Great Lakes, you can have direct light very deep. Fishermen just have to take an educated guess to get started, preferably using at least two different color patterns to begin: one for direct light and one for indirect light conditions.

Blue water

In shallower water, the background upon which the fish view the lure will be a light blue. In deeper water the background will transform to a dark blue. So, pick hues that contrast with the background—dark hues against light backgrounds and light hues against dark backgrounds.

In direct-lighted, *cold* water use combinations of silver plate, gold plate, white, blue, fluorescent green and fluorescent chartreuse. If in spawn staging areas where the fish have schooled to enter streams add fluorescent red (pink or orange). One of my favorite spoons is gold plate with a green chevron decal, as yellow gold is a long range color, and contrasts with the blue ocean background. Many saltwater spoons are chrome on nickel, but they are not bright enough lures to be as effective as silver plate.

Remember, plugs are not silver or gold-plated, but vacuum-plated with aluminum. It may look bright, but it is not as bright as plated silver. If the plug is gold, it has a yellow-colored substrate covering the aluminum. These plugs scratch easily and lose their reflectivity. To increase brightness you must oversize these plugs. Avoid prism tapes, unless you really know what color you have under water. In designing spoons, I use tape chevron decorations, but I check them out in my underwater simulator first.

In indirect-lighted, *cold* water use a fluorescent chartreuse lure with dark chevron decorations. You could also use a fluorescent chartreuse and fluorescent light blue combination. Or, a hot fire tiger decoration, which is fluorescent chartreuse, fluorescent green and fluorescent orange.

In *cool* water applications, tone down the lure's brightness by using gold plate or polished brass in combination with darker hues.

Seldom do you encounter *warm* in northern fisheries as the fish find cooler, deeper water or colder spring water. This not only gets them in cooler waters, but reduces the sky's brightness at the same time.

In the southern and inshore saltwater fisheries, you could encounter *warm* water conditions while trolling. Normally when the water is *warm*, it is summer and the sky is bright. Now is the time to avoid bright lures, and they must be toned down markedly. So stick with dark hues. There are dark plugs on the market, but few dark spoons. I would use brass or nickel plated spoons or some platinum blue, green, red or black plates.

Green water

Most *green* trolling water will be in the northern environs, from glacial melt, algae blooms and so on, but ocean water can become very green at times. The operative colors are silver, luminescent white, fluorescent chartreuse, fluorescent red (orange or pink) and

black. Most of this trolling will be relatively shallow as fish will move from conditions where they cannot see well.

In *cold* shallow water you would use silver plate with chartreuse and fluorescent red decorations. As you run deeper, you would use luminescent white and fluorescent red or fluorescent chartreuse with fluorescent red decoration. Black would work well as the water warms and the sky is bright.

Turbid water

There are tea-colored lakes where trolling is practical, but the sight

Gorden Thompson. Markeer.

distance will be limited, and we should use colors that can be seen at a maximum distance. Use combinations of gold plate, black and fluorescent chartreuse. With bright skies, go to a mostly black lure with chartreuse decoration. On dark days, fluorescent chartreuse or gold with black decoration work well. In spring, lakes can be turbid from the spring run off.

Other Considerations

Backgrounds

Fish can view lures from several directions. A horizontal viewpoint means one of our three basic water colors will determine the background and, depending upon the sky's brightness, the water will be lighter or darker in color. When fish view lures below them, it is usually a dark background except where you would have a clean sandy beach. When fish view lures overhead they are looking at the mirror-like underside of the water's surface if the water is calm. Generally, looking upward to the sky will be bright. If it is sunny you will want a dark lure, like green, blue or black with contrasting light decorations. If it is cloudy, gold will contrast better with the sky than silver and white, and of course your decoration should be a contrasting darker color.

Night time, noon time, brightness control

Night fishing—from dusk to dawn—can be productive fishing time. Fish are comfortable foraging on bait shelves in the shallows as *brightness* is not a factor. Bass have regular foraging routes they travel in the shallows. As mentioned, a fish's eye changes to night vision, and sees shades of gray and black quite well. The operative colors are dark blue, black and luminescent white or combinations thereof. You need not worry about any other colors. Of course, you do not want to use light-colored lures as the fish cannot see them against the lighter nighttime sky.

When there is a full moon, fish at night, particularly in the summer, when the water is *warm*. During the day the fish will be deep and/or undercover depending upon water clarity.

While in Austin, Texas, I fished Lake Austin weekly year round. I fished with a young friend, Jody Jackson, who was absolutely the best bass fisherman I have ever known, and a local fishing celebrity. He began fishing Lake Austin when a teenager. He could skip cast under boat docks with a casting reel, something I never learned competently. Lake Austin is a clear water reservoir in rocky country. Weeds grow on the lake bottom at thirty feet due to the bright summer Texas sun. We always caught most of our big fish between 11 am and 2 pm. Why? Because after the early morning bite on bait shelves, the bass would head for cover and bunch up under the best shade—boat docks and stalls. We would skip cast black weedless jigs under the docks and catch lots of fish while others had left the lake during the midday sun.

I fished tea-colored Lake Fork one summer day with two field testing guides and a colleague. I was the only one fishing black jigs deep and bouncing them over submerged logs. Others were fishing crankbaits and spinner baits. I caught eight nice bass and the most anyone else got was two. So, it does help to know how to fish in *warm*, *turbid* water, with the right *color* lure and using the brightness factor to your advantage.

Knowing a fish's habits relative to *brightness* is a must in becoming a master angler.

Gin clear water

We have mentioned that the light levels under varying condition can range over a very wide range. But when the water is "gin clear," the fisherman must do some extraordinary things, as distractions are amplified, and fish must modulate light levels by moving to deep water. A few lakes are gin clear year round, as are spring fed waters in Florida, some alpine lakes after spring thaw, and rivers and lakes when it has not rained for a long time and the water is low. The lures appear brighter than normal and even in *cold* water, the fisherman must tone down his lures and fish deeper. The conditions are exacerbated further when the sun is shining or there is no chop on the water. The first step is to downsize the lure and use as light a leader or monofilament as practical. If that does not do the trick, tone down lures from *cold* to *cool* or *cool* to *warm* or fish at night.

The term "structure" was popularized in the 60s and 70s by Buck Perry, "the father of structure fishing." Buck Perry was the Educational Editor of *Fishing Facts* magazine for years, and was a prolific writer and educator. He single handedly educated millions of fishermen on the habits of fish and how they relate to structure. Perry's premise, and a correct one, was that "the home of fish is in deep water." He traveled the country demonstrating the worth of his structure fishing methods. He developed the Spoonplug™ and promoted it widely. The spoon plug is a metal spoon with a bill on which Perry developed a trolling methodology. His first book[19] *Spoonplugging...Your Guide to Lunker Catches*, is the primer of structure fishing. For more information on the subject visit www.americaoutdoors.com/spoonplugger. Forty years after Buck Perry's breakthrough approach to fishing, structure fishing is a household word.

Structure is any anomaly on the bottom to which fish relate. It can be a shoal, an outcropping, a ridge, a break in the bottom—that is, any change in the bottom that provides a sanctuary or a pathway to which a fish can relate. *Structure* is usually identified by perusing contour maps, which now abound in tackle shops. The important thing to realize is that this is a behavioral phenomenon and is explained by our discussions in Chapter Two. Fish relate to *structure* because of the conditioning process; they are conditioned to recognize home and the pathways to and from home.

First and foremost, fish need a sanctuary where they are protected from predators. They need a place where light penetration is not too bright. They need cover in which they can wait in ambush. Their home sanctuary may have a shoal of fish in it, with its normal pecking order, and mixed species. From their sanctuary they take foraging excursions along the structure, which has guideposts along it. These guideposts take the form of boulders, stumps, creek beds, submerged roads, boat channels, points, islands, and so on. The fish learn these pathways along the structure and can navigate outbound

Jason Cates.
Silver salmon.

and inbound. In other words, fish must always relate to something, and they learn their environs well.

My guess is "schooling" is a way of fish creating their own structure in open water and is a protection and foraging strategy. From a statistical viewpoint, schooling fish have a better chance for survival than being solo.

Would it surprise you to know that fish can tell time, as well as navigate? We turn to Reebs[20] for a review of what the latest behavioral research has shown:

"Night anticipation, food anticipation, time-place learning, and sun compasses have been documented in all vertebrate classes, not only in fishes. The internal clock involved is likely to be more or less the same in all; it is the circadian clock, the one that runs spontaneously with a periodicity of approximately 24 hours. (Circadian comes from the Latin *circa*, or "about" and *dies*, "day.")

"Aside from the circadian clock, there is another timing mechanism that some fishes may have. It is one that they share only with those few animals that live along shorelines. This clock runs at a periodicity of approximately 12.4 rather than 24 hours, which corresponds of course to the duration of the tide cycle. Such a clock is said to be circatidal, and it allows an animal to anticipate high or low tide events."

Besides being aware of the time of day, fish are good navigators, because of knowing the time of day and the position of the sun. Knowing the position of the sun is referred to as a sun-compass. "In fact, ethologists know that the clock of fishes can be consulted more or less continuously throughout the day. This is because they know that fishes possess a sun-compass mechanism that allows them to find their way back home when they get lost." Sun-compass orientation has been demonstrated in at least a dozen species of fish, such as

Mike Sheldon.
Bluegill.

Jamie Hendricks.
Rainbow trout.

sunfish, bluegill, largemouth bass, and sockeye salmon.

Anyone who has fished for stripers knows they are great navigators. Each day they follow a forage route for miles, and pass the same structure every day at approximately the same time. Good striper fishermen leapfrog the stripers and intercept them at various locales depending upon the time of day.

Salmon and brown trout navigate by olfactory sensors during spawning runs. I fished the Piedra River in Colorado, and the brown trout would migrate up the San Juan river into the Piedra from their home sanctuary lake in upper New Mexico to spawn in the fall. Kokanee (landlocked sockeye) spawn in rivers that flow into their home lakes, and they navigate by olfactory sensing too, just like their sockeye brethren in the ocean.

The Texas Fish and Game Department has used telemetry to monitor lunker bass in the summertime. They generally leave their home structure in the evening and run a prescribed route onto a food shelf to feed. The round trip takes hours, and large bass can haunt the same locale for years or until the environs change. They usually stay within a range of a couple hundred yards of home. They are making the trips at night, so bright sun is not a problem, and they can forage in the shallow with safety.

In this chapter, we have touched on elements of another good cognitive ability of fishes: the capacity to orient properly in a vast expanse of water to find home. To help their way around, fishes can recall the scent of home, learn the visual landmarks that characterize home, listen for sounds of home, and figure out geographical direction based on their sun compass.

So, the more you know about fish, the more fascinating they become. Next let's explore the subjects of barometers, dog days, cold fronts, moon phases and tides, and see how they relate to fishing.

Karl Koeppel.
Brown Trout.

Barometers, dog days, cold fronts, moon tables and tides

Barometers

The variable that has the most influence on fishing success is weather. You do not have to be a weather expert, but some weather basics will go a long way to getting yourself on the water in the most productive manner. Obviously, you want to be off the water during storms, when the water is white capping and unsafe, but unless it is downright miserable, weather should be no excuse for not enjoying a day on the water. Of course, fishing can be easier under certain conditions, but you seldom have the luxury of good weather all the time. I have won bass tournaments after cold fronts, caught limits of bass while it was snowing, and caught king size rainbows when the temperature was below freezing. Many times a good rain shower has stimulated the fish to action. So, it behooves the serious fisherman to know a respectable amount about the weather. Obviously rain makes the rivers flow and fills the lakes. A fresh rain (called a "freshet") starts the salmon upstream to spawn. Many of us at home have the Weather Channel on TV to consult, but when you are out camping on a lake for a week, it does little good. And it is always nice to know when a cold front is approaching, which means amongst other things that the wind will blow hard for a spell. Of course we all know the importance of water temperature and have a thermometer in our tackle boxes, but for a long stay on a lake a barometer would not be a bad idea.

The average pressure exerted by the atmosphere is approximately 15 pounds per square inch at sea level. Pressure is registered in inches of mercury on a barometer. The standard sea level pressure expressed in these terms is 29.92 inches at a standard temperature of 59 degrees Fahrenheit. As altitude or temperature increase, barometric pressure decreases. Because the sun heats the atmosphere unequally, differences in pressure result, which cause a series of neverending weather changes.

If you look at a barometer, you will see that the top of the dial reads around 29.75 inches. For every increase in 1000 feet of altitude above sea level the barometer reads one inch of mercury less. So a 29.75 mid scale indicates a barometer is set for around 170 feet in altitude. A strong high pressure system will register around 30.9 inches, and a deep low pressure system will read around 28.95 inches. Exhibit 2 indicates how rates of change of barometer readings predict weather changes. Exhibit 2 is worth a study to see how changes in barometric pressure are precursors of tomorrow's weather.

Many fishermen believe that barometric changes directly affect the behavior of fish, but that is not correct. The mercury in a barometer is 13.6 times heavier than water. So, for a major swing in

Exhibit 2

Weather Forecasting[1]

Wind	Barometer*	Character of weather
to NW	30.10 to 30.20 and steady	Fair, with slight teperature changes, for 2 to 2 days.
to NW	30.10 to 30.20 and rising	Fair, followed within 2 days by rain.
to NW	30.20 and above stationary	Continued fair, with no decided teperature change.
to NW	30.20 and above, falling slowly	Slowly rising teperatures and fair for 2 days.
SE	30.10 to 30.20, falling slowly	Rain within 24 hours.
SE	30.10 to 30.20, falling rapidly	Wind increasing with force, rain within 12 to 24 hours.
o NE	30.10 to 30.20, falling slowly	Rain in 12 to 18 hours.
o NE	30.10 to 30.20, falling rapidly	Increasing rain and wind within 12 hours.
NE	30.10 and above, falling slowly	In summer, with light winds, rain may not fall for several days. In winter, rain within 24 hours.
NE	30.10 and above, falling rapidly	In summer, rain probably within 12 to 24 hours.In winter rain or snow, with increasing winds, will often set in when barometer begins to fall and the wind sets in from NE.
o NE	30.00 or below and falling slowly	Rain will continuw 1 to 2 days.
o NE	30.00 or below and falling rapidly	Rain, with high wind, followed within 36 hours by clearing and in winter, colder.
SW	30.00 or below and rising slowly	Clearing within a few hours and fair for several days.
E	29.80 or below and falling rapidly	Severe storm imminent, followed within 24 hours by clearing and in winter by cold.
N	29.80 or below and falling rapidly	Severe northeast gale and heavy percipitation; in heavy snow, follwed by a cold wave.
ng to W	29.80 or below and rising rapidly	Clearing and colder.

uced to sea level

Weather Forecasting", *The World Book Encyclopedia*, (Field Enterprises, 1963), p134.

pressure of one inch of mercury, all a fish has to do is move up or down in the water 13.6 inches to compensate. When you have wind changes, a change in light intensity and a change in raining or clearing, it is the weather change that affects the fish's behavior, and not the change in pressure per se.

Primarily in lakes, fish are affected by weather changes, particularly those involving wind. During stable weather, fish are conditioned to the environment and develop specific habits. When the weather changes, and there is instability in their habitat, they have to learn new foraging behaviors and reorient themselves. Depending upon the severity of the weather change, the water must settle and the fish must go through a new conditioning process. It is the changes in weather patterns to which the fisherman must key. When the weather is out of the northeast, forget it for a couple days until things settle down.

Dog days

"Dog days of summer" was used by old timers to claim that fishes' mouths became soft in late summer and would not bite. The warm waters of summer and the longer, sunlit days, require different tactics. Anglers schooled in Color Technology realize, to catch fish under these circumstances, you must tone down lure brightness, go to darker, smaller lures and fish deeper (or at night).

Cold fronts

Cold fronts are misunderstood by many fishermen. It is more of an excuse than anything. This does not mean that the fisherman does not have to make major adjustments. But no switch has turned the fish off. The fish have learned a successful routine for several days, perhaps a longer spell, and all of a sudden their ecology changes.

As the front passes, wind blows across a lake, forcing surface water to move towards one end, or change direction. Wind action actually causes a current in a lake, with a vertical as well as horizontal mixing effect. A predator that has taken up an ambush on a point, for example, will have to change his position, because the prey will have changed their pattern or scattered.

When a cold front passes, the sky will clear and become much brighter, and fish will go deeper and seek cover. The standard nomenclature is that the fish have "gotten lock jaw." What should be said is that the fish have relocated and our fishing pattern is now obsolete, so we have to find a new one. This will take time. Sometimes an adjustment can be done quickly—sometimes overnight, but sometimes it will take a day or two depending upon the severity of the front and the openness of the water. Sometimes parts of the lake have become turbid due to a frontal rain storm with its associated runoff. Now is the time to check the area out.

I had been fishing Toledo Bend, in Texas, for two days with a colleague, and the fish were pre-spawn to spawning. One of the best spots was an irregular bay where the fish were getting ready to spawn, and we were doing quite well. Then on the second afternoon a cold front hit and zilch. We were in a protected bay, but it changed from overcast to a bluebird sky in a very short time. Toledo Bend was starting to whitecap so we had a very rough ride getting back to the campground. It blew hard all afternoon but tapered off late in the evening. The next morning my buddy said we might as well head home as we were to leave at noon for the long drive home. The sky was clear blue. I recalled a steep bank at the entrance to our bay, and when we left it the whitecaps were breaking against that shore causing the water in the area and the bay to become turbid. I said we should give it a try if the bay was still turbid. So we ventured back. We fished right up against the shore. In turbid water, fish relate to the shoreline as a needed reference. We fished black plastic lizards and caught and released our limits by noon. Remember in turbid water and bright skies, black is the operative color.

On another occasion, I was fishing a tournament on Lake Travis near Austin, which was in rocky hill country with very clear water. We were not on the lake more than an hour when a "blue norther" hit us. We had to head for a large bay to shelter, as getting back to the ramp was impossible. The bay was protected and fishable. So, we said, we might as well fish while we wait out the storm. We took out a spinning rods with six pound test line and proceeded to limit out and win the tournament on small black hair jigs. Remember in very clear water and bright skies to go small and dark.

A couple of other neat cold front tricks are to fish on the leeward side of windy points, or get where the waves are washing ashore and cast crankbaits to the shore cover. Bait fish get overtaken by the current and are washed shoreward. Feeding bass have learned that pattern, too.

When a cold front hits, the fish are not turned off, but are having to change their foraging behavior.

Fishing after a cold front is just another fishing challenge. Remember the sky has changed from overcast, pre-frontal, to "bluebird" in a very short time. So if you persist on fishing the same places in the same way, it will indeed seem like the fish "have lockjaw."

Moon tables

Moon tables have been around for years. You can purchase a yearly pamphlet which tells you the best times to hunt or fish. They are based on the moon's position and its closeness to the earth (it travels in an elliptical orbit around the earth). So the best fishing is supposed to be when the gravitational pull of the moon and, to a lesser extent, the sun, are the highest. They even schedule bass tournaments based on moon tables.

Do these moon tables work? Perhaps—but there are so many other success factors in the equation of catching fish, how are you to tell? The aforementioned Ralph Manns made a statistical study of bass tournaments over many years. He correlated the catches in tournaments that were fished during "best periods" with those out of those periods. His conclusion was there was at best a ten percent advantage in fishing during prescribed prime periods.

My experience is that the tables indicate one of the best times to fish is when the moon is overhead at midnight and at noon the next day. Unfortunately, in the summer, the fish feed a lot at night under moonlight, and are deep and under cover at noon. As it should be, there is never an easy answer to the fishing equation, and I discarded the moon tables years ago.

Tides

Of course tides correlate with moon tables, but when we talk tides, we are referring to any fishery that is within tide water. I know nothing about blue water fishing, and will restrict my observations to fishing inshore, inlets, passages, estuaries, gulfs, and so on. I have fished the Gulf of Mexico for drum and sea trout (weakfish), and salmon, ling and halibut in Alaska. Except for the varieties of the tides, saltwater fish follow all other principles set forth in this book.

Let me paraphrase Sosin and Clark[21] the subject of tides. "To the saltwater angler, tides are not only important but may be critical. Many inshore areas only contain fish on a certain stage of the tide and then only for an hour or two. The rest of the time, the entire area may be void of fish. ...Generally speaking, if you find fish at a particular location on a certain stage of the tide, and weather and temperature do not fluctuate much, you'll probably find fish there again the next day only the time will be one hour later; the time of the next day's tide. Tides are caused mainly by the gravitational effect of the moon, and to a lesser degree by the sun. ...On new and full moons, the tides are somewhat higher and lower than they are during other time of the month. In many areas, you'll find that fishing is better during those periods because the fish can sometimes invade areas that they cannot reach under normal tidal conditions. Not only are the times of the tides important, but the tidal range or amount of rise or fall can be equally important. Fishermen look for the widest range in the tides. Top anglers are keen students of fish behavior (relative to tides)." Competent guides will "amaze their clients by staking out in a particular location and announcing that the fish will be along within a half hour. What they have done is stake out along a route normally taken by fish on a particular stage of the tide and they know by experience and observation that when conditions reach a certain level, the fish will be along." It has been noted that fishing along the shoreline "falls off sharply on the last half of the falling tide and the first part of the incoming. It's best when the water is a couple of hours before flood and for the first two hours afterward. As a general rule, if an estuarine system of bays and marshes is drained through a few narrow openings to the sea, you can always expect to find game fish waiting at the narrow inlet or channels when the outgoing tide reaches a good velocity, sweeping food from the shallow bays seaward."

Salmon, steelhead and sea-run cutthroat enter the rivers just before and during high tide. The tide gives them a good start up the river, against the current, to the first holding pools. They actually travel up the river in schools since they have all entered at the same time from schooling in the inlet.

Other than the tidal phenomenon, saltwater fish have the same physiology and behaviors as fresh water fish. They face into the tidal currents so you must adjust your presentation accordingly, but you use the same *color technology* principles in fishing for them.

9 Ponds, lakes, oceans & streams

Michael Statezny.
Walleye.

Ponds

Everyone should have their own pond. When I lived in Austin, we lived on a golf course which had three ponds on it. Before it was a golf course, it was a ranch and the owners had planted bass in two of the ponds while the third had an outlet to Lake Austin. There, you can fish year round, although it can get a bit chilly in the winter. But I fished those ponds almost every Monday, when the course was closed. You can learn more about fish behavior in this setting than you could imagine. This constricted environment is a great place to experiment and observe fish. As I mentioned before, I would catch bass in the winter in shallow water on small silver Mepps™ spinners. I learned to scale down my plastic worms to four inches in the winter, so the lethargic bass could engulf them. I would tease them on the spawning beds to observe their reactions. It takes a while, but you can stimulate a mommy bass into engulfing a pesky chunk of soft plastic. After release they returned right to their nests. It was a wonderful place to get kids started as you seldom went home skunked. Most all my fishing was with light tackle, which doubles the fun. It is a great place to experiment as you know the fish are there and where the structure is located.

Lakes

Lakes are Mother Nature's masterpieces, and I do not believe I ever fished a lake I did not like. The challenge these days is to find a lake without water skiers, jet skis and bass boats running up and down the lake a jillion miles per hour. Except for bass fishing, trolling is a very effective way to fish lakes. Bass fishermen do not think trolling is macho enough as you only need a twelve-to-fourteen-foot boat and an eight-horsepower motor. In all fairness, many good bass fishing lakes are loaded with trees, which makes them impractical for trolling. Anyway, 90 percent of the fish are in 10 percent of the water, and the trick is to find them. If you are not familiar with the lake, a good contour map to identify *structure* and actual trolling can pinpoint where the fish hang out. Trolling is a very efficient method of locating fish. To a walleye fisherman, trolling is a way of life, as walleye are nomadic and hard to locate.

Remember, "the home of the fish is in deep water" and fish only frequent the shoreline periodically for feeding. I learned this lesson well in the 60s in the shield lakes of Canada. We would have a float plane fly us in to a remote lake and drop us off with two canoes and all our gear for a week. Our first trip was a bust, as all we were doing was casting to the shoreline. The next trip we began trolling with wobbler spoons and a live minnow behind on a leader. We learned this trick by accident.

We were having lunch on an island and a storm blew up. Two of our friends hightailed it back to camp. I said to my buddy Frank Fennell, let's put a minnow behind wobbling spoon and let the wind blow us home. We had trapped the minnows overnight in a small stream. We got no more than 100 feet from the island, running our wobbler-minnow combo on the bottom, and wham we had on two beautiful speckled trout (lake dwelling brook trout, which are char). We finished our drift and caught two more. We paddled back around the loop and caught four more. Previously, we were shore casting, but the fish were in deeper water, on the bottom the whole time. From then on, fishing the shield lakes was a no-brainer. We discovered hooks that allowed us to thread the minnow on the hook shank backwards. Lake trout and large speckled trout slash the minnow first to stun it, then engulf it head first. This arrangement facilitated that process, and we missed few strikes after that.

Anyone who is serious about lake trolling should read the aforementioned Buck Perry's book on Spoonplugging. Remember all fish relate to *structure*, and are on it or near it. As Buck Perry is famous for saying, "you can have structure without fish, but no fish without structure." It's a behavioral thing. Buck Perry also said two keys to trolling are "depth and speed" control. I would suggest that *depth* can be translated in our scheme of things into *brightness* control. And, *speed* is a function of water temperature. In the case of casting, "speed" would be retrieval speed. So, we have two other

Plate 9

tenets, *depth* and *speed*, which jibe with *color technology.*

Today, downriggers and planer boards are used a lot in walleye fishing. Downriggers are used in kokanee and striper fishing too. Downriggers make depth and speed control easy when you have a smaller trolling motor. But no matter what the lure delivery system, color technology principles still apply. And fish will be at a particular depth dependent upon light intensity. Remember, optimum water temperature is particular to the species. Even in the Great Lakes you can have circumstances where a given lure can be too bright and you must tone down the lure's brightness.

Sometimes Mepps has customers going on expeditions and they give them my email address since they want to know what lures will work best. I had an email from a fellow who had fished a lake in Alaska the year before, was going back because it was such a wonderful spot, but was disappointed in the few fish he had caught. He was renting a forest service cabin with boat. I asked him what species were in the lake, what was the water color and temperature. He contacted the forest service, and they said the water was tea-colored, was in the cool range because it was in August, and it had dolly varden and lake trout in it. They even told him the level of the thermoclime. I suggested he troll and to take certain lures based on *color technology* principles. He could not wait, after he got back, to email me that, "fishing was outstanding, the best fishing he ever had in his life."

Plate 9 shows Lisa, daughter of Mepps' president Mike Sheldon, with a 43-inch lake trout caught utilizing color technology principles. The lake trout were very deep and in indirect light and were caught on Syclops™ spoon.

Oceans
Except for bottom fishing, and mooching, the majority of my ocean fishing is trolling.

Larry Breeze. Lake Trout.

Sometimes when trollers are on fish, they will stop and mooch (jigs or heavy spoons). In the case of fishing for bluefish on the East Coast, you will cast heavy spoons since blues are schooling and voracious and will hit just about anything, if it is a "high odds" color and can be seen.

It is particularly important in ocean fishing to utilize the previously discussed long distance colors, as you want the lure or bait to be seen from a very long distance. Even if you are using herring, something colorful ahead of the herring, like a Mister Twister Salmon Prop™ will improve your catch rate. One of the great fun experiences in the ocean is fishing the "jumps," when salmon have cornered bait fish. The seagulls will tell you where to go. Much the same is fishing the "jumps" for stripers.

The ocean provides great depth to modulate light intensity. I watched a TV program where they were trolling for salmon off the coast of Vancouver Island. It was a "bluebird" sky day and they were not catching fish at 175 feet, where they had the day before. They radioed a companion boat, which was catching fish—at 200 feet. The difference 25 feet of salt water made in filtering sunlight was the difference between success and failure.

One of the better long distance colors in *cold* water is silver plate. Unfortunately, silver plate tarnishes in saltwater and is not used, plus it is more expensive to manufacture. Most bright saltwater lures are chrome or nickel plated. It takes a light meter reading to realize that they are not nearly as bright as silver plate, see page 47. As this book is being written, we at Mepps are developing a saltwater finish which will facilitate the use of silver plate in saltwater.

Plate 10 shows Mike String, Mister Twist field staffer, with a trophy saltwater redfish.

Plate 11 shows Mike Nelson, on Northern Lights out of Seward, with clients that all limited out with only two Mepps Syclops Lite™ spoons

Plate 10

Plate 11

that I had selected for him a couple days earlier.

Plate 12 shows Nick Brigman, owner of Hidden Basin Lodge on Kodiak Island, and a 20-plus-pound silver salmon caught on a green and silver prototype Mepps™ trolling spinner.

My experience with ocean trolling is that you do not need to use cut herring, or dodgers and the like ahead of lures or cut bait. If you select the right color, size and brightness of the spinner or spoon, the fish will see it from a distance and focus directly on the lure. In all my trolling experience, a proper lure, all by itself, substantially out-fishes other methods. The trick is proper lure selection.

Remember in oceans, at depth and indirect lighting, your best lure will have a fluorescent chartreuse or "glow" white base to it.

Remember to fish across the tidal current or with it. Speed is critical and you may need a sea drag when fishing with the tide or else a very small trolling motor.

Streams

The major difference when selecting lures for streams (rivers and creeks and in between) and lakes is current. In moving water, fish must conserve energy. They cannot spend much time in fast-moving water without rest. The lowest velocity in a stream is close to the bottom. This, plus the reduced light intensity is the reason they spend the majority of their time near the bottom. Summer steelhead, that spend months in the stream before spawn, eat little and frequent low velocity pocket water most of the time to conserve energy. Of course water is far less rapid in the pools, but except for insect hatches, most of the food traverses along the bottom. Remember, there is some current along the bottom, but it is much faster near the surface. You must

Plate 12

Mark Moncrief. Kokanee.

select a lure that gets to the bottom quickly and stays there. I spend much of my time fishing spinners, and if the spinner is not ticking the bottom, I am not fishing.

Stream fish face upstream or opposing the tide to hold position against the current, and to observe approaching bait. Therefore the lure must travel downstream into the fish. By feeling the spinner tick the bottom I know I am down on the bottom where I should be. To accomplish this, I cast upstream or quarter cast and tumble the spinner into the fish. My son, the fly-fisherman, casts downstream and mends the fly into the fish. Most times he has on a sinking tip and or some very small split shot to get to the bottom. Different strokes for different folks. Sometimes fish will move out of the pools into riffles and their tailouts when nymphs are washing down stream or hatches are occurring. Large rocks and boulders are great ambush points, as the fish can save energy and get some shade.

Because streams are basically shallow waters, controlling the brightness of the lure is critical since the fish are depth limited. Over a season's fishing you can go from the large, bright cold lures in the winter or spring to the small, dull warm lures in late summer.

Steelhead fishermen fish "pocket water" where the current depth and speed are just right for resting on their journey upstream to spawn.

Plate 13, shows author and son Mike with "double" rainbows using "cold and cloudy" Mepps™ Sea Best spinner at ice out.

Plate 13

If you wait for fish to "bite" because they are hungry, you will wait a long time between action. The sole purpose of a lure is to stimulate the fish so it will react to the lure, whether it is hungry or not. We saw in Chapter Two, Fish Behavior, that fishing is the process of stimulating fish to action, based on their conditioned responses. In other words, a lure is a package of stimuli. We know that fish are not stimulated by a particular color, but a lure's color and decoration allow it to be seen against a particular background. Size, shape, and motion are stimuli that must be seen by the fish. I would rank motion as a critical attribute. Sound and smell are the two other stimuli that lures can generate. Sound and smell can stimulate a fish to a state of alertness, but in the end, the lure must be seen. Any lure is more effective if it can signal vulnerability and distress.

Let us now look at conventional types of lures and see how their characteristics match up with *color technology* as well as depth and speed control. We will review spinners, spinnerbaits, spoons, crankbaits and plugs, jigs and soft plastics.

As we have seen, spinners have a lot going for them. Their bodies and blades can be plated with silver, gold and other metals and their blades can be decorated with paint. They vibrate at natural bait frequencies. They can be viewed appropriately from all four sides, and show a "stroboscopic effect" as the blades

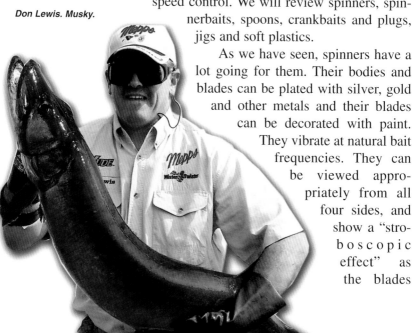

Don Lewis. Musky.

rotate around their bodies. Depending upon the blade and body combination, they can be fished at various depths and speeds. They can be trolled or cast. Plate 14 illustrates nine basic Mepps™ spinners and their application.

Spinnerbaits are a safety pin arrangement with the blade attached by a swivel to a piano wire that is connected to a separate body which usually has a slitted plastic skirt around a single hook. They are used effectively in the spring for bass and for pike and musky. They are essentially weedless and provide good vibration and flash. Unfortunately, there are hundreds of manufacturers of them and most are of poor quality. *Color technology* is not on their

	Deep Running XD
	World famous Aglia spinner
	See Best Steel head & salon
	Thunder Bug, to hatch the hatch
	Spin Flex, combination jig & spinner
	Black Furry
	Aglia Streamer
	Aglia Long for deep running
	Flying C, heavy for long casts
	Musky Killer

Plate 14

radar screen and I have to modify mine to suit. I have never found a silver-plated blade on one, and gold-plated blades are a rare commodity. Manufacturers are now camouflage painting the blades in fishlike patterns, which is ridiculous. Spinnerbaits are primarily for casting in trees, brush and cane, and can be very effective in *cold* water if fished appropriately. Unfortunately, you do not see them in *warm* water color schemes, except in my tackle box.

Spoons have been around for a hundred years or so, and there are reasons. They are simple, inexpensive and catch fish. They are easy to cast and troll, and good quality ones are available from Acme Mfg., Mepps and Daredevil. Here again, there are many cheap spoons of questionable quality on the market, which are usually nickel or chrome-plated and inappropriately decorated. Many use colored tape indiscriminately, and the makers have no idea what the spoon looks like under water.

Crankbaits and plugs have been around for ages and until recently were made of wood. Now they are made of hard plastic. Casting crankbaits is my favorite way of bass fishing. Of course, most crankbaits float, and you have to crank or troll it down to depth. Unless you are using downriggers, you need about five sizes of a crankbait to be a complete crankbait fisherman for depth control. My favorite crankbait series is the new Timber Tiger™ by Tom Seward. You can get information on it and how to fish crankbaits effectively at www.yakimabait.com. Crankbaits are most effective in *cool* and *warm* water as they cannot be silver and gold-plated like metal lures. One of my all-time favorite lures is the Flatfish™ which can be trolled slowly behind a canoe, gives off great vibrations and can be manipulated to act like wounded prey. If you are selective, you can find a few crankbait models that are decorated to fit *color technology* criteria. Stay away from fancy, lifelike (camouflage) decorations.

Jigs have been around for ages, too, They are very versatile and fit many applications. Because the heads are made from lead, most are painted, as they cannot be plated. But if you are selective, you can find or make some that fit color technology criteria. By the right color combinations of head, skirt and soft plastic grub, you

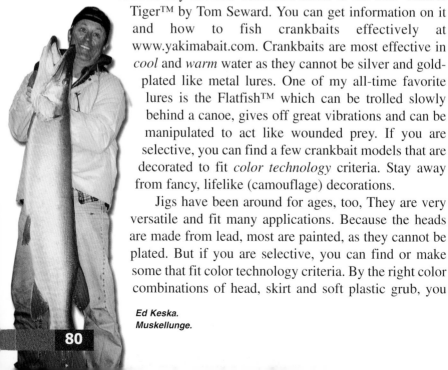

Ed Keska.
Muskellunge.

can have a "light on dark, dark on light" scheme with contrasting colors. A popular way of steelheading is fishing jigs under floats. And the good steelheaders tie their own jigs with silver and gold beads on the head and achieve excellent *cold* water decoration. (They also float fluorescent pink four inch plastic worms under a float, as it is bright and effective in *cold-green* water). "Jigging" generates good visual stimulus.

From a *color technology* standpoint, soft plastic-using bass fishermen have a long way to go. I have made talks to many bass clubs, and bass fishermen pursue questionable avenues when it comes to color selection. They have blanket rolls full of all kinds of plastic baits in a wide variety of colors and configurations. They go out of their way to find exactly the right color worm (or lizard, or some other creature) with the right colored flakes in it. I call it the "magic color syndrome," and it makes no sense. Most fish have only two sets of rods and cones in their eyes, while humans have three. Fish can see the colors their prey reflect well, but beyond that someone is putting the shuck on you. The majority of bass fishermen are convinced that fish are color selective and prefer a particular color, which does not hold up under scientific scrutiny. Fish are not like women buying purses and shoes. On the other hand, fish can be negatively conditioned to avoid certain colors if continually "stung" by a lure of a particular color. However, if a tournament is won with a chartreuse worm with a red and green flake, everyone runs out the next day and buys them all up. Little do they know that the green and red flake turn black under a few feet of water (which by the way is good for overcast turbid water conditions).

Like all lures, you really do not need many combinations for soft plastic. I fish with four plastic colors, and that is it— no point in wasting money and filling up tackle boxes.

John Aschembrenner. Tiger Musky.

At one seminar I had the host bring in several of the most popular colored lizards. He did and I put them in my simulator. Guess what, they all looked the same under water. There are so many plastics manufacturers using so many different dyes and flakes that I really do not know how to get a handle on this one. I get my Exude™ plastics from Mister Twister, in a few colors, and have a deaf ear to all the new "hot colors" that crop up all the time. Plastic grubs make great spinnerbait and jig trailers, and by contrasting the head colors, you can have an effective combination of colors. If fished "Texas style" or "Carolina rig," you can fish plastics on the bottom where you belong.

Lures are just a bundle of stimuli that must be seen by the fish and that the fisherman must deliver at the right depth and the right speed. It takes a lot of time on the water to get all you can out of a lure. So, select one, and get very good at fishing it before moving to another. There is more than one way to catch a fish. And, part of the battle is to have confidence in your lure selection and presentation, so if the fish are there you will get them. Yes, selecting the right lure is critical, but fishing it properly is essential too.

Walter Lightbourn.
Northern Pike.

Mark Plath.
Walleye.

The "right lure" by itself will buy you little if you are not "on the fish." Knowing everything you can about the water you are fishing sets the stage for success. Being a *structure* fisherman builds on your knowledge of the water. You also must practice *depth* and *speed* control fishing techniques. I know of nothing better than fishing one body of water frequently and knowing it like the back of your hand.

In the Introduction, we used the term "high odds" lure. "Low odds" lures will catch fish once in awhile, when by luck you are fishing a particular lure when the conditions are just right. We have learned that lure selection is the last thing we do after we have the appropriate data on water and sky conditions for the body of water we will fish. Remember, a particular lure will only be a "high odds" lure under specific conditions. So, determine the conditions, then pick the lure and the right combinations of colors and brightness.

Choosing the right lure is a three step process:

Step 1
Appraise the fishing conditions:
Light Levels—whether the sky is Sunny, Cloudy, Rainy or Low Light.
Water Temperature—whether the water is Cold, Cool or Warm (Exhibit 1)
Water Color—whether the water color is Blue, Green or Turbid/Stained.

Step 2
Determine the background upon which the fish will view the lure:
Refer to Illustration 4 and select the background upon which the lure will be viewed.

Step 3
Choose the basic lure color combinations and brightness that contrast with the background selected in Step 2. See the Operative

	Salmon	Steelhead	Trout(lg)	Trout(sm)
S/PKGR				
Cold/Cloudy	#5	#4	#3	#2
S/GRPK				
Cold/Sunny	#5	#4	#3	#2
G/BKGR				
Cool/Cloudy	#4	#3	#2	#1
BK/CHBK				
Cool/Sunny	#4	#3	#2	#1
TB/GRBK				
Warm/Cloudy	#3	#2	#1	#0
COF				
Warm/Sunny	#3	#2	#1	#0
S/BKGL				
Low Lt/Cold	#5	#4	#3	#2
Low Lt/Cool	#4	#3	#2	#1
Low Lt/Warm	#3	#2	#1	#0
GB/BKCH				
Turbid/Cold	#5	#4	#3	#2
Turbid/Cool	#5	#4	#3	#2
Turbid/Cool	#4	#3	#2	#1

Plate 15

Colors and "brightness guides" Chapter Four, pages 46 and 47. Also, refer to Plates 15, 16, 18 and 19 for examples.

We have mentioned the importance of *depth* and *speed* and speed control. Here is where the geometry and mechanics of the lure come into play. In the case of spinners, spoons, crankbaits and plugs, each design should function properly in a given depth range over a given range of speeds. If you are fishing crankbaits, you need about five models for different depth ranges. Fortunately, crankbait manufacturers usually specify the depth the lure will run with a given thickness of line. As noted, Mepps has different spinner designs for *depth* and *speed* control. If you are using downriggers, which set the depth, then you need lures that suit the range of trolling speeds. For downriggers, you want light lures whose depth does not vary as speed is changed.

In 1998, in consultation with Colin Kageyama O.D., the writer and Mepps R&D developed the See Best™ line of spinners. This was the beginning of Mepps Color Technology which now permeates all our lure design efforts. The name See Best was coined to support the design criterion that fish can "see best" this spinner under specific water and sky conditions. This line of spinners was developed originally for steelhead fishing in rivers, but is exceptional for salmon and trout too. Colin teamed up with Mepps, as there was no equal to the Aglia blade for steelhead fishing. Because

			Body/Blade/Bead
Cold/Cloudy	S-S	Silver/Silver/Red
Cold/Sunny	G-S	Gold/Silver/Fl. Green
Cool/Cloudy	G-G	Gold/Gold/Fl. Green
Cool/Sunny	G-BK	Gold/Black/Fl. Green
Warm/Cloudy	GR-TB	Green/Tarnished Brass/Fl. Green
Warm/Sunny	BK-BK	Black/Black/Blue
Low light	BK-S	Black/Silver/Glow White
Turbid	BK-G	Black/Gold/Fl. Chartreuse

Plate 16

of the way expert spinner fishermen cast to steelhead in "pocket" water, the See Best™ spinner has incorporated a unique body design so the spinner is seen from all directions. It was designed for quarter casting and tumbling the spinner into the fish along the bottom. And, tape decorates the backside of the blade to be seen by the steelhead as the spinner swings into them. All in all, it's a serious spinner for the serious river fisherman.

Plate 15 shows the eight See Best™ color combinations, each designed for a specific set of river conditions. This selection matrix starts with selecting the species and water temperature. When the water is *cold*, the water is usually snow melt or runoff. When the water is *cool*, it is usually late spring or fall. When *warm*, it is usually in the heat of the summer, and the water is low and clear. Note how brightness is "toned down" as the water warms. Note the tarnished brass and coffee bladed models, something you will not find in other lines of spinners. Note too, the models for "turbid/muddy" and "low light" conditions.

Because of the water I fish, the Mepps XD™ (extra deep) is my standard stream spinner. I fish a lot of larger, faster rivers, and I need to get to the bottom. I spent two summers in Colorado testing the XD before we took it to market. It is an extraordinary stream spinner. The shaft through blade design is well suited for mountainous rivers. The combinations of body, blade and bead allow us to follow the "light on dark, dark on light" decorating principles. In Plate 16, I show you my selection of the eight color combinations that constitute my base *color technology* set. I can catch fish anywhere, anytime with this set. If I know the water temperature before I go, I need only four spinners for the day.

Plate 17

One of the most underutilized lure colors is black. I guess the color is not sexy enough, or bright and shiny enough. You seldom see them in spinners and spoons. They are available in crankbaits and plugs, but are rare on the shelves. However, in Texas, they have a saying about plastic baits: "I don't care what color I use, as long as it's black." This is because of the very bright sun and warm water in summer, and because a lot of the reservoirs' waters are stained due to submerged timber. It is counter intuitive, but black is also the best all-round night color. Most metallic blues and greens are seen as black by the fish in *clear* water.

Here are some *black* conditions:
- When the water is relatively warm and clear and it is sunny.
- When the water is turbid or stained and it is sunny.
- When the water is green and it is sunny.
- When the water is gin clear. (Go black and small.)
- At night, when fish's eyes adjust to the night and can discern dark hues.
- When fishing on the surface, especially at night.

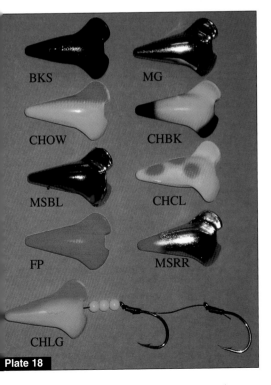

BKS

MG

CHOW

CHBK

MSBL

CHCL

FP

MSRR

CHLG

Plate 18

A good exercise for the student of *color technology* is to judge the lures in your tackle box and figure out in what conditions they are best suited. Ask these questions: In what color of water will it best be seen? In what water temperature is it suited? Upon what background will it be viewed by the fish? Is it for sunny or cloudy conditions? Will the fish view the lure from below? Is it suited for deep indirect light conditions, or must it be in direct light? What you will probably find is that most of your lures are "high odds lures" in a very narrow range of applications. It is not the number of lures you have, it is the proper mix of colors and brightness that matters.

Now let's look at lures that are mostly color, in this case, the Mister Twister Prop™ which is used on halibut and ling cod in Alaska, salmon in the northwest and walleye across the States. Plate 17 shows Jason Cates, a Mepps field staffer, with a near Alaska state record ling cod. Note the super PROP™ that was used to give visibility to the "halibut rig."

Plate 18 exhibits nine PROPs™ in various color combinations. See their application in Appendix 1.

Now, as a final exercise, let's examine an array of eighteen Syclops spoons, Plate 19, and decide as to what fishing conditions they individually apply. So that you can test yourself, we have the answers in Appendix 2.

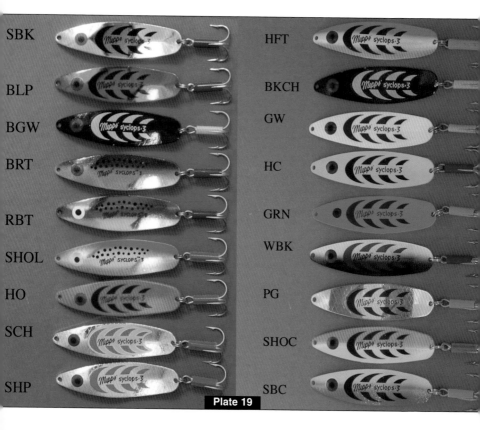

SBK · HFT · BLP · BKCH · BGW · GW · BRT · HC · RBT · GRN · SHOL · WBK · HO · PG · SCH · SHOC · SHP · SBC

Plate 19

When you look at a lure and know what conditions it matches with, you are on the way to becoming a master angler. And, your catches will improve markedly, just like mine did when we developed the color technology process.

Without *color technology* techniques you will always have two nagging questions. Do I have on the right lure or am I not on the fish? By selecting the "high odds" lure for the conditions, you can fish with confidence and spend all your time in zeroing in on the fish. Because we are creating contrast between the lure and the viewing background, fish can see the lure from a greater distance. Instead of having to "hit the fish on the head" with your lure, you have much greater latitude to stimulate the fish to strike, and thus can cover much more fishing area. I have seen bass come a good forty feet to hit the right colored lure. I have also seen trout follow my lure for a great distance and never take it as it was too bright for the conditions.

I have purposely gone into much detail in this book. My son Mike says, "Dad, I just asked you what time it is, you don't have to tell me how to build a watch!" Well, I knew of no better way to convince the reader that the color technology system works than to show that it has a firm foundation based on a thorough knowledge of fish and how they behave, backed up with careful research proven over many years of fishing. I hope I have given you the fundamental underpinning to sort through all the hype that exists in the tackle industry and allow you to read fishing articles with a framework to judge their worth. I know that after the first read of this book, when you begin to apply its principles, you will be on the path to becoming a "Master Angler." And that makes me feel that our journey was worthwhile. Keep this book by your side, and I'll see you on the water.

Chris McGrath.
Striped bass.

Jason Cates.
Silver salmon.

APPENDIX 1

Prop Model	Light Level	Water Temp.	Water Color	Back-ground	Remarks
BKS					
MG	Sunny to	Cold/Cool	Blue	B1 B2 B3	
	Rain	Cold/Cool	Turbid	T2 T3	
CHOW	Cloudy	Cold/Cool	Green	G2 G3	
	Cloudy	Cold/Cool	Blue	B2 B3	Short Range
CHBK	All	Cold/Cool	Turbid	T2 T3 T4	
MSBL	Cloudy	Cold/Cool	Blue	B1 B2	
CHCL	Cloudy to	Cold/Cool	Blue	B2 B3	
	Rain	Cold/Cool	Green	G2 G3	
FP	Overcast	Cold/Cool	Blue	B2 B3	Short Range
		Cool	Green	G2 G3	
MSRR	Overcast	Cold/Cool	Blue	B2 B3	Short Range
		Cold/Cool	Green	G2 G3	
CHLG	All	Cold/Cool	Blue	B1 B2 B3	Long Range
		Cold/Cool	Green	G2 G3 G4	

APPENDIX 2

Syclops Model	Light Level	Water Temp.	Water Color	Background	Remarks
SBK	Cloudy	Cold/Cool	Blu/Grn	B2 & G2	
	Low light	Cold/Cool	Blu/Grn	B3 & G3	
BLP	Overcast	Cold	Blu/Grn	to B2 & G2	
	Low light	Cold/Cool	Blu/Grn	to B3 & G3	
BGW	Sunny	All	Blu/Grn	to B4 & G4	
	Low light	All	Blu/Grn	to B4 & G4	
BRT	Cloudy	Warm	Blu/Grn	to B3 & G3	
RBT	Cloudy	Cold	Blue	B2	Spawning
SHOL	Cloudy	Cold	Green	G2 & G3	Spawning
HO	Cloudy	Cold	Blu/Grn	to B3 & G3	Spawning/ Short Range
SCH	Cldy/Sunny		Cold	Green	to G3
SHP	Cloudy	Cold	Blu/Grn	B3 G3	
HFT	Sunny/ Cldy	Cold/ Cool	Blu/Grn	to B3 & G3	Multipurpose
BKCH	Sunny	All	Turbid	to T3	
	Low Light	All	All	to B3 G3 T3	
GW	Low Light	All	All	to B4 G4 T4	
HC	Any	Cold/Cool	Any	B3 thru T4	
GRN	Any	Cold/Cool	Blue	B1 B2 B3	
WBK	Low Light	Any	Blue	B1 thru B4	
PG	Sunny to Rain	Cold/Cool Cold/Cool	Blue Turbid	B1 B2 B3 T2 T3	
SHOC	Cloudy	Cold/Cool	Green	G2 G3	
SBC	Cloudy to Rain	Cold	Blue	B1 to B3	

ENDNOTES

1 P.H. Greenwood, *A History of Fishes*, (New York, John Wiley and Sons, 1975), p 151.

2 Stephan Reebs, *Fish Behavior in the Aquarium and in the Wild*, (Ithaca and London, Cornell University Press, 2001), p 43.

3 P.H. Greenwood, *A History of Fishes*, (New York, John Wiley and Sons, 1975), p 171.

4 Stephan Reebs, *Fish Behavior in the Aquarium and in the Wild*, (Ithaca and London, Cornell University Press, 2002), p 47.

5 Paul C. Johnson, *The Scientific Angler*, (New York, Charles Scribner's Sons, 1985) , pp 25-45.

6 Stephan Reebs, *Fish Behavior in the Aquarium and in the Wild*, (Ithaca, Cornell University Press, 2001) p 11.

7 Richard W. Mallot and Donald L. Whaley, *Psychology*, (New York, Harper and Rowe, 1976), pp 294-295.

8 Richard W. Mallot and Donald L. Whaley, *Psychology*, (New York, Harper and Rowe, 1976), pp 102-112.

9 Dr. Loren G Hill, "Bass and Color", *Bass Fishing Techniques 92*, p 17

10 Tom Seward, "WHAT BIG BASS EAT," *Fishing Facts,* February 1992, p 65.

11 Mark Sosin and John Clark, *Through the Fish's Eyes*, (New York, Harper and Row, 1973), p 89.

12 Mark Sosin and John Clark, *Through The Fish's Eye*, (New York, Harper & Row, 1973) pp 162-163.

13 Joseph S. Levine and Edward Fl MacNichol, *Color Vision in Fishes*, SCIENTIFIC AMERICAN, February 1982.

14 Joseph S. Levine and Edward F MacNichol, Jr., "Color Vision in Fishes", SCIENTIFIC AMERICAN, February 1982.

15 Colin J. Kageyama, *What Fish See*, (Portland, Frank Amato, 1999).

16 Phil Rabideau, *The Colors Fish See Best*, MEPPS 1999 Fishing Guide, pp 30-31

17 Mark Sosin and John Clark, *Through the Fish's Eyes*, (New York, Harper & Row, 1973), pp 108 - 120.

18 Darryl Choronzey, *VIEWING FISH In Their Own Realm*, Salmon-Trout-Steelheader, June-July 2000, p 57.

19 E.L.Perry, *Spoonplugging...Your Guide to Lunker Catches*, (Hickory NC, Clay Printing Co, 1973)

20 Stephan Reebs, *Fish Behavior in the Aquarium and in the Wild*, (Ithaca, Cornell University Press, 2001) pp 93-108.

21 Mark Sosin and John Clark, *Through the Fish's Eyes*, (New York, Harper & Row, 1973), pp 190 & 191.

Index

More Hancock House titles:

Steelhead
Barry M. Thornton
ISBN 0-88839-370-9
5½ x 8½, 192 pp.

West Coast Fly Fisher
Compiled by
Mark Pendlington
Contributing author:
Barry M. Thornton
ISBN 0-88839-440-3
5½ x 8½, 152 pp.

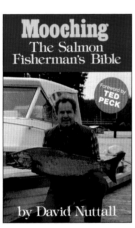

Mooching:
The Salmon
Fisherman's Bible
David Nuttall
ISBN 0-88839-097-1
5½ x 8½, 184 pp.

Saltwater Fly Fishing
for Pacific Salmon
Barry M. Thornton
ISBN 0-88839-268-0
5½ x 8½, 168 pp.

Trout Fishing
Ed Rychkun
ISBN 0-88839-338-5
5½ x 8½, 120 pp.

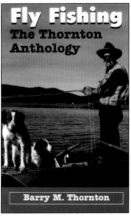

Fly Fishing
The Thornton Anthology
Barry M. Thornton
ISBN 0-88839-426-8
5½ x 8½, 191 pp.

Fishing Hot Spots
of the Upper Fraser Valley
Richard Evan Probert
ISBN 0-88839-307-5
5½ x 8½, 96 pp.

West Coast Steelheader
Compiled by
Mark Pendlington
ISBN 0-88839-305-9
5½ x 8½, 96 pp.

Guide to Salmon Fishing
Ed Rychkun
ISBN 0-88839-305-9
5½ x 8½, 96 pp.

**How To Catch
Really Big Fish**
Tara Robinson
ISBN 0-88839-967-7
5½ x 8½, 64 pp.

**195 Lakes of the
Fraser Valley Vol. I**
Ed Rychkun
ISBN 0-88839-339-3
5½ x 8½, 238 pp.

**195 Lakes of the
Fraser Valley Vol. II**
Ed Rychkun
ISBN 0-88839-377-6
5½ x 8½, 272 pp.

**Bar Fishing the Lower
Fraser River**
Hugh Heighton
ISBN 0-88839-237-0
5½ x 8½, 80 pp.

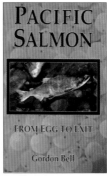

Pacific Salmon
From Egg to Exit
Gorden Bell
ISBN 0-88839-237-0
5½ x 8½, 128 pp.

Salgair
A Steelhead Odyssey
Barry M. Thornton
ISBN 0-88839-412-8
5½ x 8½, 96 pp.

HANCOCK HOUSE PUBLISHERS
1431 Harrison Avenue, Blaine, WA 98230-5005
(604) 538-1114 • **Fax (604) 538-2262** • **www.hancockhouse.com**